Remodeling Your Kitchen and
Building Your Own Cabinets

Remodeling Your Kitchen and
Building Your Own Cabinets

by Virginia T. Habeeb
and Ralph Treves

Drawings by Lloyd Birmingham

POPULAR SCIENCE BOOKS

Acknowledgements

The authors acknowledge with sincere thanks the generous cooperation of the following groups and individuals: American Home Lighting Institute; Assoc. of Home Appliance Mfg. and their members; American Institute of Kitchen Dealers and their members; Edison Electric Institute; Gas Appliance Mfg. Assoc. and their members; Home Ventilating Institute; Major Appliance Consumer Action Panel; National Assoc. of Plumbing, Heating and Cooling Mfg.; National Home Improvement Council; National Kitchen Cabinet Assoc. and members; U.S. Department of Agriculture; Dr. Rose Stiedl, Cornell University; H. Peers Brewer, Manufacturers Hanover Trust Co.; friends, professional associates, agencies that supplied photos and technical data.

Cover setting courtesy of Baths by Royal

Library of Congress Catalog Card Number: 74-33571
ISBN: 1-55654-004-3

Seventh Printing, 1987

Manufactured in the United States of America

Contents

Introduction to Part I

The kitchen may be the most important room in the house. It is where you prepare food, where your family and friends often gather, where you perform such important household chores as sewing, potting plants, arranging flowers, laundering. In short, the kitchen is the life center of the home.

In Part I of this book we talk about remodeling your kitchen so it will function efficiently as a life center. To accomplish this, we'll bear in mind Frank Lloyd Wright's famous dictum that "form follows function." That is, the design of a kitchen is determined by the tasks that you have to perform there. We won't slight the all-important matter of eye appeal. We know that attractive surroundings make us feel good and happy, and inspire us to do our best work. With today's colorful materials, it is not difficult to make a kitchen attractive. But, above all, a kitchen must be functional.

The first chapter in this book shows you how to evaluate your present kitchen and establish guidelines for transforming it into a better one. We even give you a short time-and-motion study to help you create a layout of maximum efficiency. Then we discuss the various alternatives available to you: minor alterations; remodeling in stages; major remodeling. And we suggest seven ways to finance the job.

Kitchens can be grouped into a number of different categories. We explain the basic styles and shapes that a kitchen can take, how to plan around obstacles, and how to design what we call an "efficiency triangle." Then we discuss decorating options, evaluate materials available for floors, walls, ceilings and windows, and explain how to develop a harmonious color scheme.

The best way to achieve a functional kitchen is by designing it around work centers based on major appliances. We discuss these work centers at some length and suggest how they can be incorporated into your kitchen design.

Once the basic design of the kitchen has been established, it's time to talk about cabinets, countertops and appliances. Cabinets can be built on site, ordered from a dealer or custom-made in a shop to your own specifications. However you obtain them, they are the key to a kitchen's storage efficiency. We list the types available and show a variety of storage facilities from different manufacturers. Appliances, too, must be carefully chosen. When remodeling a kitchen, you must decide which appliances you wish to keep and which to replace. To help you evaluate new appliances, we include a special check list and give you a rundown on the convenience features of each.

When you've done all the planning and purchasing, the time comes to install cabinets, countertops and appliances. If you want to do the job yourself, you'll find step-by-step illustrated instructions for cabinet installation. If you prefer to give the job to a professional, we tell you what to expect from him and what he expects from you. A chart lists all the types of kitchen specialists and describes their services.

Finally, we explain how to design an energy-efficient kitchen. This can be done. It's just a matter of shopping intelligently for appliances. The FTC has begun a labeling program that rates the energy consumption of appliances. We analyze the system and show you how to evaluate appliances for maximum energy efficiency.

Planning a kitchen can be a creative and satisfying adventure. We hope the first part of this book serves as a useful guide to transforming your present kitchen into the room of your dreams.

Virginia T. Habeeb

PART I | REMODELING YOUR KITCHEN

1 A New Kitchen— The Possible Dream

IN OUR INTRODUCTION, we established that the kitchen has emerged as perhaps the single most important area of the home—the hub around which our entire lifestyle centers. It is indeed a multipurpose center, and so it is not enough simply to install cabinets and appliances along four walls and call it a kitchen.

Let's focus first on what you want in your new kitchen. It is easier than you think to have a better, more attractive and functional kitchen. But it will make it even easier if first you answer some important questions. We have devised key check lists to help you analyze your present kitchen and then determine what changes are necessary to transform it into the kind of kitchen you really want—and need.

YOUR PRESENT KITCHEN. Determine what you like and don't like about your present kitchen. Study the scorecard below to rate your kitchen. If you are planning to remodel, you'll soon find out where you want to make changes. If you are building a new kitchen from scratch, then you'll have a better idea of how to go about planning the perfect one for you. First, take time to think and study, then plan.

Scorecard

How does your kitchen rate? Find out by scoring it from 1 (poor) to 6 (good) points in each of the categories listed below, circling the appropriate number. Add the point total and check it against the scorecard * below.

1. Storage Space. Is there enough? Is it easily accessible or are there hard-to-reach corners? Do you need a stepstool to get at the top shelves? Have you space to store portable appliances, cleaning supplies, trays and serving utensils?   1 2 3 4 5 6

2. Work Space. Are surfaces convenient for food preparation? Have you 24 inches of counter space on each side of the sink? A 15- to 18-inch "landing space" adjacent to the refrigerator door handle? An 18-inch safety area alongside the cooktop?   1 2 3 4 5 6

3. Lighting. Is there adequate task lighting for the sink, range and counters? Is general lighting properly directed so you don't work in your own shadow?   1 2 3 4 5 6

* Scorecard provided through the courtesy of the American Institute of Kitchen Dealers.

4. Appliances. Are yours up to date? Do they in-   1   2   3   4   5   6
clude a dishwasher, frost-free refrigerator, self-
cleaning oven, microwave oven, trash compactor,
sink with garbage disposal facility? Have you such
conveniences as built-in toaster, can opener, warming drawer, instant hot-water dispenser?

5. Ventilation. Is it adequate to remove moisture,   1   2   3   4   5   6
odors, and to prevent grease deposits on cabinets,
windows and walls? Is the vent hood approximately
21 inches above the range, where it operates most
efficiently?

Add the numbers you circled and enter the total
of 1–5 here. (   )

If your total is:

4-10 You are working daily in an obviously inadequate kitchen.
11-15 Your kitchen has major shortcomings that could (and should) be
corrected.
16-20 Your problems aren't serious; still, a remodeling would be beneficial.
21-25 Your handicaps are minor and probably easily resolved.
26-30 You are fortunate. Yours *must* be a good kitchen!

How did you rate? Chances are, if you were really honest with yourself, you
found that you are living with problems you didn't even know existed. It's easy
to get used to doing things the same way each day without realizing that possibly there could be a better way, an easier method.

TIME AND MOTION. If you really want to get technical about this kitchen remodeling, why don't you take a lesson from the time and motion experts? Using
a pedometer, they compute the number of steps it takes to perform a certain
task and clock the time it takes to do it. Then they analyze the methodology by
answering such questions as:

1. Am I wasting any time?
2. Is there an easier method?
3. Is there an appliance or utensil that will make the job easier, quicker?
4. Can I cut the job out entirely?
5. Is my equipment in proper working order?
6. Are supplies readily accessible?
7. Is there a way to simplify the task? Should I change the working arrangement or sequence, tools, equipment, body position or motion?

With honest answers to these questions, you can then set about finding a better way or designing a more functional kitchen.

YOUR OWN TIME AND MOTION STUDY. Select a certain task—preparing dinner, for example. Attach a pedometer to your waistband and check the number of steps it takes and the time it takes to do it. Then ask these same questions in an effort to find a better method.

It might be fun to do and, besides, you will learn something about how you work. Do this enough times as you work, even without a pedometer, and it will soon become second nature for you to analyze how you work and to seek ways to improve your working habits. Certainly, it will help you to plan a more efficient and workable kitchen—a dividend you'll be thankful for in years to come.

Or, if you don't really want to get that technical about it, walk through a task on paper as we have done for a dinner party. It will help you to accomplish the same thing.

Consider the typical preparation of a dinner party for eight on an average Saturday evening. Walking on paper first through the preparation of a menu is a good way to determine how a kitchen can function, short of doing the actual thing.

THE MENU

Jellied Consomme with Sour Cream

Cheese Straws

Roast Beef

Glazed Onions   Buttered Peas

Salad   Vinaigrette Dressing

Orange Ice Parfait   Cookies

Coffee

Note: If freezer compartment is not large enough to hold parfait glasses, change dessert.

Preparation time is 1¼ hours in advance and one hour on the evening of the dinner. (Preparation time may be planned as convenient to hostess' lifestyle.)

10:00 A.M. Prepare and cook celery. Hard-cook egg for salad dressing. While celery and eggs are cooking, wash lettuce leaves for salad.

Refrigerator to sink to range; back to refrigerator to sink

When celery is almost tender, turn off heat and cool.

Refrigerator center

Range center

10:20 A.M. Make vinaigrette dressing. Cover and store in refrigerator. Put 3 cans of consomme in refrigerator. Cut one lemon in 8 wedges. Refrigerate. Remove orange ice from freezer to soften.

Refrigerator center

10:35 A.M. Set table—place mats, dinner plates, salad plates, silverware, wine and water goblets, napkins, salt and pepper, carving set, centerpiece. Have ready—soup cups and saucers, serving platters and dishes, dessert glasses, coffee cups and saucers.

10:55 A.M. Spoon orange ice into parfait glasses. Place at once in freezer. — Refrigerator center

11:10 A.M. Remove celery from broth and refrigerate. — Range and refrigerator center

11:15 A.M. Finished with pre-preparation.

6:00 P.M. Put beef in open roaster in 325° oven. — Oven center
Arrange flowers and put on table. — Dining center
Put consomme in soup cups; refrigerate. — Refrigerator center
Peel onions and put on to simmer. — Range center

6:15 P.M. Melt butter in saucepan for glazed onions; add sugar, salt and pepper. Turn off heat. Drain onions; 15 minutes before serving, place in saucepan with melted butter. Meanwhile prepare peas and heat. — Refrigerator and Range center

Put cheese straws on plate on table; cookies on sideboard. — Dining center

Add minced egg to salad dressing. — Refrigerator center

6:30 P.M. Shower and dress.

7:00 P.M. Set up coffee maker. Place celery on salad plates; garnish with lettuce leaves. Shake dressing and pour a little on each celery head; refrigerate. — Refrigerator center

7:20 P.M. Organize cocktail area; put out appetizers, ice bucket and glasses. (Time dinner according to length of cocktail hour.) — Serving center

7:30 P.M. Top consomme with sour cream. Add lemon wedges on side. — Refrigerator center
Check roast and adjust timing. — Range center
Relax with guests. — Living center

Most of the preparation for this dinner party is concentrated on the refrigerator and sink centers. If these areas are more than 7 feet apart (see page 24, The Efficiency Triangle), you can waste steps, time and energy. If utensils are not stored in areas where they are used, there is more waste of time and motion.

Research has shown that simple reorganization of a kitchen can save 500 steps in the preparation of dinner alone—from 700 steps to 200 steps. If this is so, just think how much time and energy you can save by working in a well-planned, efficiently arranged kitchen.

This kitchen has custom-designed wooden cabinetry with base and wall units in contrasting styles. Other features include a brick wall with a ventilated, recessed cooking hearth and rotisserie, built-in ovens and a central island sinks. Beamed ceiling, wall-covering and floor-tile border add decorative notes. *Courtesy Wood-Mode.*

HOW WILL YOU USE YOUR NEW KITCHEN? What did you find out about your kitchen? Are there many things you'd like to change? If so, then you are on your way to knowing exactly what it is you really want in a new kitchen.

Next, it's time to analyze yourself, your lifestyle and your family needs. Who are you and how do you like to work?

Rose Steidl of Cornell University has this to say about Functional Kitchens: "Kitchens planned for the *worker* as well as the *work* that is done are functional. A kitchen planned for the worker means less effort. You can work easily because those things that make a difference have been taken into account."

What is it that makes a difference to you? To find out something about yourself and your family, use the check list below. Rate yourself and your family lifestyle. In this way, you'll have an idea how best to determine the things that make a difference to you and how best to incorporate them into your new kitchen plan.

YOU AND YOUR FAMILY LIFESTYLE CHECK LIST. Find out by scoring the following items with a YES or NO. For every YES answer you have, you've a positive point to incorporate into a new kitchen plan. These are the items that make a difference to you and which take high priority in your future planning.

Every NO answer indicates a low-priority item in your new kitchen plan. This is your check list to better decision-making, a more functional kitchen.

Will you plan for:
( ) ADDITIONAL COOKS
( ) HUSBAND
( ) CHILDREN

Will your children help you cook or cook by themselves? Does your husband enjoy cooking as a hobby? Will you want to plan for additional sink area, counter space, duplicate utensils?

( ) AN AREA FOR VISITORS IN THE KITCHEN WHEN YOU COOK

Are you a gregarious cook, or would you rather be alone? If you don't mind guests while you cook, provide an area for them to sit while you cook—a snack bar or a small table—away from the mainstream of cooking activity. If you do not want to encourage visiting, plan a small cooking area for you alone.

( ) KITCHEN DINING

Will you eat most of your family meals in the kitchen or need a place just for breakfast or short-order snacking? If most of the meals are served in the kitchen, you'll want to plan for an adequate dining area with enough space to allow family and friends to sit and move about easily. If your kitchen is used only for occasional snacking or quickie breakfasts, a dining bar or snack counter may be adequate.

( ) A PLAY AREA FOR CHILDREN

If you have preschool youngsters to care for (or occasional visiting grandchildren), you may wish to plan a special area for them so you can "watch while you work."

( ) ENTERTAINING ACTIVITIES

Will you have dinner parties often or occasionally? What type of entertaining do you prefer—large parties, small ones, casual or formal? If you entertain large groups frequently, you'll want to plan additional storage space for party platters, utensils, extra dinnerware. You'll also need ample refrigeration area, freezer space, pantry storage and countertops. And you may want to consider the duplication of utensils, appliances and other items.

( ) OTHER ACTIVITIES

What activities other than cooking might take place in your kitchen? Herb growing, gardening, hobby participation, sewing, laundry, buffets, kaffee-klatsching, writing? A kitchen lends itself to many associated activities, *if* you plan the space for it and provided you have the space to plan.

( ) A DECORATING THEME

Most likely, you'll want to decorate your kitchen to reflect your tastes and your family lifestyle. Consider your tastes. Do you prefer conservative colors and patterns, or will you opt for bright, exciting designs and motifs?

Simplicity is the keynote in this kitchen. Natural light wood cabinetry with matching veneered recessed panels offer both enclosed and open shelving. Every inch of shelf space works for you—even the area between wall and base cabinets, over the countertop. Ceramic tile backsplash and matching floor tiles coordinate beautifully with the oak cabinets and bar stools. *Courtesy Allmilmo.*

Now is the time to let it all out! If you've ever wanted this or that, at least include it in your thinking plans. Of course, plans change as final thoughts take shape, depending upon limitations of space, money and availability of materials. But do go all-out now. It will help you determine priorities.

PLANNING GUIDELINES. A good kitchen takes a lot of thought and planning. And a certain amount of daydreaming and window-shopping. A good kitchen always follows basic planning principles, but a super kitchen is one that includes the planning principles and all the personal details you have listed, clipped, jotted down, collected and sifted out in your "dream" file of ideas.

We promised to take you step by step through all the elements of kitchen planning, from the dreaming stages right down to the finished kitchen, whether you have someone else do it or will do it yourself.

Let's start with the following guidelines. Jot down the 6 steps and use them as your guide in achieving the kitchen you picture in your mind.

1. List all the things you plan to do in your kitchen. Consider every activity that might take place there. List every detail, even the smallest—menu-planning, watching television, laundering and, of course, all the attendant activities of cooking, dining and clean-up—in order of their importance to you.

2. List all the conveniences you would like to include in your kitchen. This incorporates appliances, utensils, equipment and similar items.

3. Decide how much money you would like to spend. If your budget is limited, plan some alternatives, such as doing some of the work yourself, building your own cabinets, or remodeling in stages.

4. Start a clip file. Begin early to collect pictures and ideas from everywhere—magazines, books, booklets, brochures, information from cabinet and appliance manufacturers, leaflets from utility companies and from your local extension service.

5. Design several kitchen plans you might want to consider and settle on your favorite one. Draw the final plan as accurately as possible, following the instructions in Chapter 8. When you have done this, you will be in a better position to explain your needs to a professional kitchen designer, kitchen dealer, or a builder, if it is in a new house. Or, if you are going to complete the remodeling yourself, you will be prepared with the basic plan.

6. If you do not plan to do the job yourself, begin early to shop around for qualified, reputable kitchen dealers or contractors who will do the work for you. Talk to them, compare notes, explain your needs, get estimates, floor plans and as many suggestions as you can. The more information you have the better the decision-making process.

A kitchen with a host of ideas: refrigerator door and dishwasher front coordinated to match cabinetry; corner oven installation; table built around work island—ideal for the cook who wants to visit with guests. Clever placement of convenience outlet at table allows use of portable cooking appliances. *Courtesy Wood-Mode.*

An L-shaped kitchen with a center island helps to confine food preparation to the area. Lower counter provides special place for dining, menu planning or other tasks. Oak ceiling beams complement cabinetry while easy-care vinyl brick flooring and ticking-type wallcovering tie it all together. *Courtesy Haas.*

YOUR KITCHEN IDEA CHECK LIST. As you begin to think about your new kitchen, fill out this check list first, so you won't overlook any of the latest conveniences. Take this, along with your plan, to your kitchen dealer or designer who, with this information in hand, will be better able to create the ideal kitchen for you.

I would like the following appliances:

( ) Built-in Wall Oven	( ) Trash Compactor
( ) Built-in Cooktop	( ) Refrigerator
( ) Freestanding Range	( ) Freezer
( ) Microwave Oven/Range	( ) Ice Maker
( ) Ventilating Fan and Hood	( ) Washer
( ) Dishwasher	( ) Dryer
( ) Garbage Disposer	( ) Other

I prefer the following cabinetry:

( ) Wood	( ) Plastic
( ) Metal	( ) Combination wood and metal

Slate-like, laminated countertop lends an authentic note of nostalgia to this kitchen. Contemporary convenience features include the cooking island with a custom-styled hood that facilitates food preparation and serving in the adjacent dining area; wall-mounted can opener; corner mixer cabinet with a slide-up door and plenty of hidden specialty storage. Coordinated checkered wallcovering and curtains add a decorative note, while soffits, ceiling beams and vinyl "brick" flooring wrap it up from head to foot. *Courtesy Mutschler.*

The cabinetry styling I prefer is:
- ( ) Colonial
- ( ) Traditional
- ( ) Contemporary
- ( ) Provincial
- ( ) Mediterranean

I would like laundry facilities in my kitchen: _____Yes _____No.

I would like eating facilities in my new kitchen for _____ persons.

I plan to do a great deal of entertaining: _____Yes _____No.

I would like to consider the following convenience areas:

( ) Plan Desk   ( ) Sitting Area
( ) Flower Arranging   ( ) Family Room Design
( ) Barbecuing   ( ) Sewing Area
( ) Bar Sink   ( ) Other

I prefer a:

( ) Single Bowl Sink   ( ) Stainless Steel
( ) Double Bowl Sink   ( ) Porcelain Enamel

I would like to have the following special cabinets and accessories:

( ) Cutting Board   ( ) Pantry Cabinet
( ) Towel Rack   ( ) Cutlery Drawers
( ) Linen Cabinet   ( ) Slide-Out Refuse Can
( ) Bread Box   ( ) Spice Cabinet
( ) Broom Cabinet   ( ) Pull-out Table
( ) Tray Storage Cabinet
    Others: _____

I need storage facilities for the following special items:

_____

_____

2 | Financing Your New Kitchen

YOU MAY HAVE in mind exactly what you want in a new kitchen. No doubt, you have listed with abandon all the things you have dreamed about as you have thought about your new kitchen. Or you may have some very set ideas about what you want to change in your present kitchen. Whatever the case, it is important that you have a good idea at the outset of just how much the total job will cost in order to determine what you can actually do. With few exceptions, most of us need to budget our expenses for major expenditures.

Just what you do finally and how much it will cost depends upon how much work is involved, exactly what kind of work it will require, the quality of materials you choose—from less expensive to very expensive—how many frills you plan to include, and whether or not you will have someone else do all the work or leave some for yourself.

REMODELING ALTERNATIVES

1. Minor alterations. This is what I like to call cosmetic surgery or giving your kitchen a face lift. You can spend as little as $200 for some open shelves over a worktable and gain $2000 worth of efficiency. Or, you can change the mood of your kitchen setting and improve the environment and ease of maintenance by sprucing up the walls with washable wall covering. Or, you can increase your cooking efficiency immeasurably by simply installing a microwave oven, for example, to save time and effort.

2. Minimum remodeling. For a basic kitchen, this means some new cabinetry, new countertops, new appliances and minor face lifts here and there—a new floor or wall or window treatment. Structural changes, if any, should be kept to a minimum.

3. Major remodeling. This includes necessary and practical structural changes—adding on a room, extending or moving a wall, changing doors, windows, radiators and/or plumbing. In such cases, you probably will not stint; you'll do whatever has to be done to improve your kitchen design. Plan also to change the flooring, wall treatment and most of your appliances, if necessary. Install new cabinets with added convenience features and include other areas, such as dining, sewing, planning, barbecue or family room centers.

4. Remodel in stages. If your budget is minimal, plan to acquire your new kitchen "on the installment plan." Do some of it now and some of it later.

It's a good idea to design the entire kitchen from the beginning, however, and map out your step-by-step strategy according to your budget and a predetermined time schedule. Determine your priorities. If you don't have the money for a dishwasher now, for example, install the countertop, but leave space underneath for its future installation. For now, slip a stool under the counter and use the space as a sit-down work area. Plan all your electrical and plumbing changes in the first stage. Special financing may be arranged for this type of remodeling. Your local bank may be able to provide information about the ramifications of unit-by-unit remodeling.

If you opt for stage-by-stage remodeling, make a list of your preferences. You may decide that you really need a new refrigerator, and that instead of new cabinetry, a new coat of paint is all that's needed to spruce up your present ones, or that your dining table and chairs should be refinished.

An Example of Unit-by-Unit Modernization

1st Unit. Remodel wiring and electrical system. Install new cabinetry and range.

2nd Unit. Install dishwasher. Add new kitchen table and chairs (for dining and additional work surface).

3rd Unit. Install new lighting, flooring and paint woodwork. Add wall covering.

Some Tips on Saving Money

- Shop carefully and buy only what you need. Avoid appliance models, for example, which include features you may never use. Purchase energy-efficient appliances.
- Plan to have other repairs, such as plumbing or wiring, needed in the house done at the same time kitchen remodeling is taking place. This can reduce labor costs immeasurably.
- Design your kitchen to utilize present plumbing facilities, if possible. Avoid long and costly pipe runs or changing plumbing locations.

5. Building a new house. Go all out in the kitchen, insofar as your budget permits.

THE BUSINESS OF PAYING. Financing your kitchen remodeling may be easier than you think. Let's analyze the cost of a new kitchen in several different ways.

The Association of Kitchen Cabinet Dealers tells us that, individually, about what you'd pay for a car you'll invest in a kitchen. Today, a typical kitchen remodeling may cost around $4500 to $5500. This is for a basic remodeling, which includes new cabinetry, new countertops, some new appliances and perhaps a minor face lift here and there. It does not involve major structural changes or complete modernization of wiring and plumbing—only minor changes.

It is not unusual to find many homeowners borrowing for home improvement remodelings, particularly kitchens. Today, the business of borrowing money for kitchen remodeling is considered practical in the face of inflation and rising costs. Besides the added, increased convenience and pleasure it affords the homeowner, a complete kitchen, new or remodeled, can increase the resale value of any home anywhere from 10 to 15 percent.

If your credit profile is satisfactory and/or the bank has appraised (and approved) your home, financing a new kitchen should be easy.

Financing may be arranged through a kitchen dealer or contractor, although you can probably make better terms on your own through some form of lending institution—a bank, finance company or credit union. Many times a dealer or contractor who does arrange financing for you may ultimately "sell his paper" to the bank for financing, and this could cost you more than you bargained for.

If you are in the market for financing: (1) Determine exactly how much your financial needs are; how much the improvements will cost. Then, (2) investigate the avenues of financing through your bank, local finance company, kitchen dealer or contractor, your credit union or some other lending institution.

Generally, you have about seven choices for financing kitchen improvements.

SEVEN CHOICES FOR FINANCING KITCHEN IMPROVEMENTS

HOME IMPROVEMENT LOAN

The amount of money a bank will lend depends on your collateral, credit profile and ability to repay the loan. You can obtain up to $15,000 on a loan of five to fifteen years' maturity for 10 to 13 percent annual rate of interest. The amount of the loan may vary depending upon geographical location and institution. How much actual money you receive depends upon the method the bank uses to compute the interest rate, either by the *add-on* or the *discount* method.

In the discount method, the interest is deducted from the total amount at the time the loan is initiated and you receive the remaining amount. In the add-on method, finance charges are added to the face amount so you receive the full and desired amount. Ask your bank about unit-by-unit modernization for remodeling in stages.

For purposes of comparing interest rates, however, lenders are now required to also disclose rates to consumers in terms of an Annual Percentage Rate. This enables you to shop around for the best rate, comparing apples to apples.

FHA TITLE I PROPERTY IMPROVEMENT LOAN

This is a government-insured loan offering up to $10,000 for a period of one to seven years at an annual percentage rate of about 12 percent. Longer term FHA loans may be possible at lower interest rates, but they are becoming increasingly more difficult to obtain because of mounting interest rates and tight money.

REFINANCING A PRESENT MORTGAGE

You may secure a new mortgage for the outstanding balance of your existing mortgage, and an additional amount for your new kitchen needs. Plan to pay increased interest on the outstanding balance and new closing costs. If you have an older mortgage, you will be exchanging lower interest rates for today's higher ones.

PERSONAL OR COLLATERAL LOAN

Here you may obtain small cash amounts for short periods at high interest rates. Collateral is secured until the loan is paid.

SAVINGS ACCOUNT PASSBOOK LOAN

Use your passbook as security for a low interest loan.

CREDIT UNION LOAN

As a member of a credit union, you may be entitled to obtain a loan at lower interest rates.

CASH

Cash is usually paid in installments—an initial deposit, a second one when materials are delivered, a third halfway through the project and a final one upon completion.

3 | The Kitchen Shell

BEFORE WE DISCUSS the technical aspects of designing a workable kitchen plan, it might be a good idea to take a look at some of the categories or types into which most kitchens fall; then consider carefully all the elements that comprise the shell of the kitchen itself, such as the shape of the room, the floor, walls, ceilings, windows, accessories, color and lighting.

BASIC TYPES OF KITCHENS. We have found that generally there are about five basic types of kitchens. Chances are that one of those listed below will suit your lifestyle and will serve as the springboard for developing your own design.

1. The no-frills kitchen. This one is a small, no-nonsense plan which includes only the basics. This kitchen is primarily designed for food preparation and clean-up and rarely includes other centers, such as dining, sitting or laundry, though they may be nearby. If you prefer not to have too many people in the kitchen at one time, consider the no-frills design. It doesn't mean it has to be a small room; it could be part of a larger area, yet separate.

2. The kitchen-breakfast room. This kitchen has a combination breakfast-dining area. Although used primarily for cooking, it also contains facilities for dining, such as a dining table and chairs or a snack counter.

3. The open kitchen plan. It's large, open and comprised of multiple centers and often flows from one open area to another—the patio, pool, terrace, family or living room. If you have a large family, have teenagers, entertain frequently and have the space, perhaps you'll want to consider this larger, more expanded kitchen that adjoins or is adjacent to many of the public areas in your home.

4. The family room kitchen. This is the kitchen plus. It is generally a large all-in-one kitchen with facilities, not only for cooking, serving and cleaning-up but also for family room, sitting, dining and entertaining, and often includes a fireplace and/or a children's play area.

5. The creative kitchen. This one goes all out to support a personal or family hobby and shows it in furnishings and decor. It might contain a lean-to greenhouse for the garden-flower lover or boast a collection of handsome copper utensils.

These are among the basic types. And, if you adapt them to your own particular needs, who knows, you may come up with a different one entirely. That's the excitement of creative planning.

This open kitchen gives onto an adjacent dining nook. Peninsula, which houses a built-in cooktop, doubles as a serving bar and a landing space for items coming out of the built-in ovens to right. There is an abundance of storage space. Basket collection, displayed on top of cabinets, is useful when serving meals. Note clever ceiling treatment and track lighting which provides spots where needed. *Courtesy designer James Foy and* Interior Design.

Parsley, sage, rosemary and thyme . . . aromatic herbs suspended to dry overhead on ceiling beams and freshly grown ones in a window greenhouse bring a fragrant quality to this sunny open-shelf kitchen. The look of paving stones is captured in the in-laid new vinyl floor. *Courtesy Armstrong:* Good Ideas For Decorating.

If remodeling is in your plans, consider your family's future needs. Will your lifestyle require a sitting area, a place for planting? Adequate storage with the installation of kitchen cabinets will supply the convenience you need. *Courtesy Sumner Rider and Associates, Inc.*

Reinforcing the botanical theme in this family room are basket stools, wicker-glass coffee table, and a floral print fabric. Plant-filled divider partially screens the kitchen and offers a display area for plants and herbs, and a center for repotting. The lattice work at the windows provides privacy yet allows maximum light through the floor-to-ceiling windows. *Courtesy Armstrong:* Good Ideas For Decorating.

KITCHEN SHAPES. When considering what you ultimately want your new kitchen design to be, it is important to take into consideration the specific space available, the shape of the room itself, what else you want your kitchen to do besides provide facilities for cooking and serving, and whether or not the kitchen area is part of a larger unit, such as a family room, or adjacent to a porch or patio.

These four basic kitchen shapes are among the most popular.

The U-shape design. This is perhaps the most popular and practical plan of all. Each work center is planned on one of three walls, with the sink center as the pivot. A common variation is a Broken-U.

Advantages

Avoids traffic congestions.

Provides continuous counter space.

Saves steps between work centers.

Disadvantages

Probably costs more.

While providing corner space for dead storage, some corner storage may be inaccessible.

Planning Tips

The back wall of the floor plan should be at least 8 feet to provide 4 feet of open floor space between the two side work area walls.

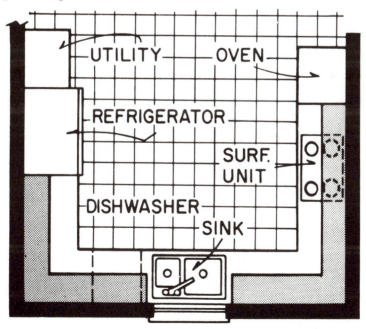

U Shaped

The L-shaped design. This is a feasible and efficient plan for two adjoining walls. A common variation is a Broken-L.

Advantages

Allows full use of the remaining walls.

Provides flexibility in placement of appliances.

Provides space for additional work centers or dining.

Continuous counter space.

Disadvantages

Increases distance between centers.

Some loss of corner space.

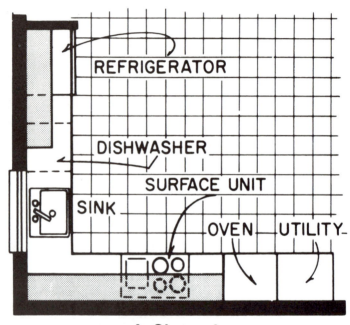

L Shaped

The two-wall or corridor design. This is suitable for a long, narrow space. You may increase the efficiency of this plan if you close one end of the room to "through traffic."

Advantages

Less expensive, no corners to turn.

Adapts easily to work patterns.

Disadvantages

Could create traffic congestion.

Too much walking between centers.

Planning Tips

Floor space should be at least 8 feet wide but no more than 10 feet.

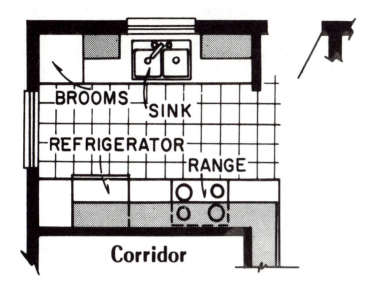

The one-wall design. This plan is frequently found in apartment kitchens or where space is at a premium, such as in vacation homes.

Advantages

Adapts well to family room or open plan.

Excellent for limited space.

Disadvantages

Fails to provide ample counter space.

Not enough efficient storage.

Could limit use of appliances and reduce convenience.

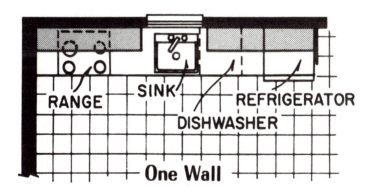

Variation planning. The flexibility in adapting any of the basic shapes is achieved through the placement of islands and/or peninsulas. Islands or peninsulas can help bring centers closer together in large, spread-out areas. Or, they can divide centers conveniently from one another. Technically, islands or peninsulas will allow more efficient use of space. The installation requires at least 4 feet of space between opposite centers or a minimum of 3 feet if a passageway.

PLANNING AROUND OBSTACLES. In almost any kitchen plan, it is not unusual to encounter pesky problems that may be seemingly insurmountable. With a little ingenuity and a lot of patience, you can easily solve some of the more common obstacles. Here are some simple ideas you'll want to note.

To make a kitchen larger. Consider combining two rooms by removing a wall. For example, expand the kitchen work area by removing the wall to a small breakfast nook.

To make kitchen areas smaller. Use islands or peninsulas to confine certain work areas, or make two rooms by placing a wall or divider to separate the kitchen from laundering facilities.

To camouflage obstacles which cannot be moved. Install cabinets around chimneys, clothes chute, heating ducts or pipes to hold brooms, trays, similar equipment.

To utilize space between wall studs. Install shelves for canned goods, utensils or other household items; or use space to store ironing board and ironing supplies; or install perforated hardboard on walls to hang pots, pans, skillets, strainers, etc. Cover the area with louvered doors, screens or decorative window shades.

To hide unsightly pipes. Box them in by extending the wall around pipes.

To camouflage radiators. Cover them with perforated metal, and paint to match color scheme; or remove a radiator if it is not used for heating.

To free wall space affected by door swing. Remove the door entirely if it is not used as a major entrance or exit.

To raise a countertop. Place plywood or similar boards of proper thickness on the floor under the base cabinet.

To lower a countertop. Use a lower base cabinet.

THE EFFICIENCY TRIANGLE. In developing the most functional arrangement for a good kitchen plan, consider the strategic placement of the three main work centers. They should be so placed to form the points of an imaginary triangle. With such an arrangement, one expends a minimum of steps in getting from one center to the other—hence, "The Efficiency Triangle." A good rule of thumb is to make certain that there is no less than 12 feet and no more than 22 feet total around the three sides of the triangle. If you plan for these minimum and maximum measurements, you should achieve a practical plan:

4 to 7 feet between sink and refrigerator.

4 to 6 feet between sink and range.

4 to 9 feet between range and refrigerator.

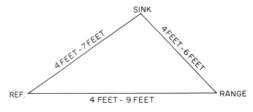

A Gallery of Modern Kitchens

This L-shaped kitchen design features a work island/snack counter and recessed, step-saving niches. Left to right: serving/work counter niche faces outdoors; work counter/planning niche with telephone and calendar provides landing space for oven items; cooking niche and built-in ovens; sink and cleanup niche. Beneath the overhanging counters is ample base-cabinet storage. No-wax sheet flooring requires routine maintenance only. Note circle of light suspended over work island/snack counter and built-in paper-towel dispenser handily installed at end. *Courtesy Armstrong.*

Cabinetry and countertop in this kitchen run the full length of one wall into the dining area. A versatile cutting board converts with a flip to a planning desk and work center (above). Valance and ceiling trim cut from wallcovering (below) help to coordinate kitchen and dining areas. Red trim on cabinet doors is cloth tape. *Courtesy General Tire.*

A bright and cheerful kitchen designed for step-saving convenience. Island in center serves as pivot for kitchen activities. It boasts a double sink and tiled surface for easy preparation and cleanup. Warm-toned wood cabinetry complements white appliances: smooth tap range in island; self-cleaning oven; side-by-side refrigerator; trash compactor and dishwasher. Patterned ceramic tile on sides of island and in laundry room create decorative interest, provide easy maintenace. *Courtesy General Electric.*

Elegant and inviting, this charming kitchen is basically an L-shape design with a center island. It has almost everything: built-in cooktop; side-by-side refrigerator; oven; triple-bone stainless steel sink; dishwasher; dining center. Above the island is a large and decorative wood ventilating hood. Handsome kitchen carpeting, soft underfoot, and acoustical ceiling tiles are guaranteed to muffle kitchen sounds. *Courtesy Rutt.*

An oasis all its own, this kitchen has three sink areas and features a computerized range and oven, a refrigerator which dispenses two varieties of juice, ice water and ice cubes through the door, and an undercounter dishwasher and trash compactor. Separate sections divide functions — cooking and cleanup from dining and sewing and laundry. Incandescent, ceiling-mounted bulbs follow lines of major kitchen area over sink and range. *Courtesy Interior Design magazine and Frigidaire.*

This natural-finished kitchen features a ceramic-tiled island with stainless-steel, double-bowled sink (note goose-neck faucet on smaller beverage sink); microwave cabinet with adjacent work counter: slide-in range; small-appliance storage unit with a slide-up tambour door; open-shelf and floor-to-ceiling storage. *Courtesy Crystal Cabinet Works.*

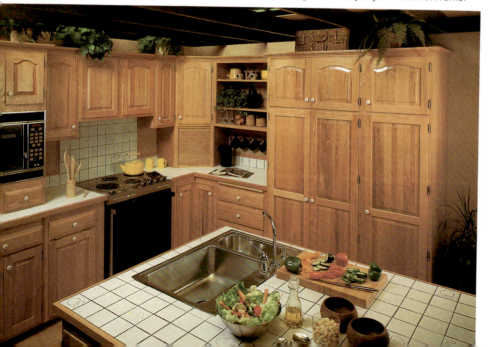

This kitchen, in a broken-L shape, is decorated with European-style cabinets, durable flooring, and vinyl wallcovering that picks up the floor colors. Counters are finished in a woodgrain plastic laminate. *Courtesy Yorketowne Cabinets and GAF Flooring.*

Here are some unique ideas worth borrowing from this updated traditional U-shaped kitchen: A disappearing open-shelf pocket pantry at the back of the U with an extra work counter that functions as a mix-bake center. Pass-through counter connects the kitchen with a family room. Fabric-covered, sliding panels, hung on ceiling tracks, close off pantry. Color scheme takes its cue from the no-wax flooring in a pattern of small orange and yellow tiles. *Courtesy Armstrong.*

Styled for urban living, this contemporary U-shaped kitchen combines earth tones with block cabinetry and a touch of blue. Ledge over the counter, open shelving and ample storage make this kitchen a joy to work in. Skylight provides light by day; ceiling and undercabinet lighting by night. *Courtesy General Electric.*

Expansive cooking island with its large hood and vent fan overhead provides this kitchen with additional storage. Ceramic-tile work surface doubles as a buffet counter for informal gatherings. Cleanup center with sink and dishwasher faces lovely outdoor view. Simple cafe curtains offer privacy. *Courtesy Interpace.*

This spacious kitchen can accommodate six teenagers and their parents. Feeling of openness is achieved with dividers. Restaurant range and grill is an aid when cooking for a large family. *Courtesy General Tire*

The outdoor theme of this pretty kitchen is enhanced by ceramic-tile floor. A half-round table at the window serves as a focal point. The island counter supports a four-burner range and a gas-fired barbecue unit. *Courtesy American Olean*.

The snack bar in this kitchen is decoratively "supported" by nautical ropes. Cabinetry is constructed with durable laminate fronts. Other features include ceramic-tile walls and floors, round twin sinks with drain basket and removable cutting board. *Courtesy Allmilmo*.

Victorian kitchen with contemporary styling takes its inspiration from leaded-glass doors in ash cabinetry. Cabinets hung over L-shaped peninsula provide pass-through to dining area. Dishwasher is elevated to waist level for easy loading. *Courtesy Maytag*.

FLOORING. It has been estimated that we spend at least 50 percent of our at-home working hours in the kitchen. This would indicate that we need something comfortable underfoot. While comfort should be the major factor upon which to base your flooring selection, keep in mind that the flooring should be a part of your decorating scheme. In making your selection, consider all the elements of comfort, ease of maintenance, safety, quality, durability and decor.

Which flooring material do you prefer? Resilient? Hard-surface? Soft-surface?

Will it be comfortable? Is it cushiony and resilient? Safe? Shock-absorbent? Smooth? Not slippery?

Is it easy to care for? Does it need waxing, or is it one of the new, no-wax vinyls? Will you find it easier to vacuum kitchen carpeting?

Resilient flooring

Sheet vinyl. This may be inlaid with the design extending throughout the entire vinyl layer. A less expensive, less durable version is *rotovinyl* with the design printed on a vinyl sheet and coated with a transparent vinyl layer. The gauge or thickness reflects cost. Look for foam-backed, cushioned vinyl, no-wax finishes.

Solid vinyl tile. This is comfortable, durable, grease, alkali and stain resistant. It is available in no-wax finishes and is easy to maintain. It is suitable for do-it-yourself installation. But, it is expensive.

L-shaped kitchen provides ample space for dining. Center table supplies additional work top for busy days. Separate two-wall plan is perfect answer to a wall jog and patterned wallcovering helps to tie two walls together. *Courtesy General Electric.*

Here's the charm of Early American with some fresh new ideas in a U-shaped kitchen. Natural wood ceiling beams, brick-faced walls and traditionally styled cabinets create a warm background. Sink center is flanked by cooking and food preparation centers. Smoothtop range is recessed in a separate, ventilated hearth-like unit, and microwave oven is installed in the brick wall. Shuttered windows, divided by a "point of interest" shadow box, transform a plain wall into an eye catcher. A patterned area rug over a wood-designed vinyl floor completes the Early American look. *All appliances from Hotpoint.*

Vinyl asbestos. This is comfortable, fairly resilient, grease, moisture and alkali resistant, and durable. It is available in no-wax finishes. It is suitable for do-it-yourself installation and is moderately expensive.

Linoleum. This is comfortable, durable, grease and stain resistant, and easily maintained, though not as easily as vinyl. It cannot be installed over concrete subflooring, but it is suitable for do-it-yourself installation. It offers limited color selection, and is moderately priced.

Asphalt tile. This has poor resistance to noise, grease and stain; therefore, it is not suitable for kitchens. However, a wide variety of colors is available and it is the least expensive.

Cork or rubber tile. Though this is durable and sound absorbent, it is not resistant to oil, grease and solvents. It is not recommended for kitchens.

Hard-surface flooring

These offer a wide variety of patterns, colors and texture, though they will be uncomfortable underfoot. If they are used widely throughout the kitchen and/or the surrounding area, area rugs with nonskid backing will help to cushion the surface.

Wood. This is available in walnut, pecan, maple, oak, birch, cherry and teak. It is durable and resilient. The new finishes have improved ease of care and maintenance, though harder to care for than vinyl. It provides a warm, natural feeling. But it requires professional installation and is very expensive.

Ceramic tile. This is stain resistant and durable. Individual tiles are replaceable. It is available in a wide selection of patterns and colors. It is suitable for do-it-yourself installation, though you must be highly skilled. It requires care and is very expensive.

Marble, quarry tile, flagstone, terrazzo, stone, brick. These have similar characteristics as ceramic tile, though noisier, and are stain-resistant only if finished with a penetrating sealer. These are very expensive.

Soft-surface flooring

These are increasing in popularity with the wide choice of colors, patterns and materials available. Kitchen carpeting is extremely soft, resilient, comfortable and sound absorbent. It reduces breakage and is easy to maintain. It is available in regular carpet widths and in tiles. Individual tiles are replaceable if damaged. Some styles are cushioned with a foam-rubber base for ease underfoot and, hence, are moisture-resistant. Jute-backed carpeting requires padding and is not moisture-resistant. It is moderately expensive.

Basic U-shape design places refrigerator/food-preparation area and self-ventilated cooking center equidistant from sink, dishwasher and clean-up area, with ample counter space for each. Service counter and separate sink area in dining center provide adequate storage for dinnerware and entertaining supplies. Note 29-inch-high counter in right foreground, used as a desk. Rail atop wall cabinets provides gallery for display of collectibles. *Courtesy Custom Craft.*

KITCHEN WALLS AND CEILINGS. It is wise to make your decisions early as to how you want to treat your walls and ceilings. You'll find such an exciting selection of wall coverings and an enormous variety of ideas for ceiling treatment that you will want to give this phase of your remodeling much thought. Whatever your decision, make sure that it blends with the rest of the decor, is easy-to-care-for and is durable.

Kitchen walls serve both functional and decorative purposes. In strategic areas they are excellent as backdrops for pegboard, hooks and shelves for hanging and placing all kinds of kitchen utensils within fingertip reach. They also play a prominent role in carrying out the decorative theme. Wall surfaces are large, generally at eye level, and one of the first things a person notices when entering a room. Treat them carefully. Wall covering, tiles, paint and paneling are among the most popular treatments. In selecting any wall treatment, keep these practical guidelines in mind.

1. Is it grease, acid, moisture and stain resistant?
2. Is it washable or wipeable?
3. Does it require minimal care?

This sleek contemporary-styled kitchen was designed for easy maintenance and step-saving convenience. It's compactly U-shaped, yet unbroken lines assure ample counter space, adequate storage. Wall between ceiling-height wall cabinets and counter is easy-to-clean ceramic tile, complemented by checkered window shade. Range hood is concealed under cabinet-like door which opens hydraulically. *Courtesy Tielsa.*

This L-shaped kitchen corner features light-finished oak cabinets, tiled backsplash wall, open shelves for easy-to-reach items, ventilated smooth-surface cooktop, built-in under-counter oven and a double-bond stainless-steel sink. *Courtesy Poggenpohl.*

Wall covering. This is one of the least expensive ways to effect a dramatic change in any room. It can alter the light quality of a kitchen, add dimension, lighten a dark room, add warmth to a cool one, emphasize color accents, complement others, highlight a focal point, de-emphasize obstacles, set a decorating theme, give your kitchen its personality.

Wall covering includes wallpaper, plastic-coated paper, fabric- or vinyl-coated fabric. In making your decision on what kind of covering to choose, consider the following:

- Your decorative theme.
- Color.
- Placement in kitchen. (If it is near a cooking or clean-up area, you'll certainly want the washable variety.)
- Permanency. (If you ever plan to remove it, consider the strippable variety. Paper-backed covering must be removed by steam, and that can be an expensive process.)

This contemporary kitchen, a perfect U-shape with a clean, unbroken line, has wall cabinets on one side only. Storage needs are met mainly by base cabinets in the cooking peninsula which open both ways. Cabinetry is of stain- and scratch-resistant melamine with flush doors, self-closing hinges and color-coordinated integral pulls. Note decorative features: diagonal wood-paneled walls; vaulted, beamed ceiling with skylight; lean-to greenhouse and countertop windows, excellent for herb-growing. *Courtesy Excel.*

Tile. This is another excellent choice for kitchen installation. It includes the *ceramic, metal* and *plastic* varieties.

Ceramic comes in a variety of patterns, colors, textures and finishes. It is resistant to kitchen stains, scratches and water. It is washable and requires very little care beyond that of wiping.

Metal tile is similar in character to ceramic, though the choice of patterns and colors is not as wide.

Plastic tile also does not offer as wide a variety of choice. It is not scratch or heatproof, though it is wipeable and easily cared for.

Paint. This is a safe decorating choice, but it does not provide the personality characteristics that other wall coverings do. Color choice is broad in that paint offers you the possibility of mixing a special color. In order to have the flexibility of easy care, ask your painter for a gloss or semigloss finish. It is washable.

Paneling. This is another possibility, and it comes in natural woods and a variety of plastic laminates.

Other treatments. These include the natural materials, such as *stone* and *brick*, which are often used when a room is extended and an outside wall can be remodeled advantageously for use indoors. Or, they can be used to highlight a rustic theme around the range or cooking area, or near a fireplace wall in a family area.

Ceilings are too frequently forgotten in planning a kitchen. They do play a prominent part in reflecting light in the kitchen and color selection should be fairly light. Remodeling ceilings is a relatively easy job with do-it-yourself, easy-installation ceilings. Some of the most popular treatments include wall covering, paint, suspended and beamed ceilings, panels and tiles. Let's discuss them in more detail.

Wall covering. It need not be confined to the wall. Continue wallpaper or wall covering on up and over the ceiling and down the next wall.

Paint. This is an economical treatment for both walls and ceilings. It should be steam and moisture resistant and easily cleaned.

Suspended ceilings. These are becoming increasingly popular. Unless you are trying to lower a high ceiling, they do lower the room height somewhat. They allow you to cover up an unsightly old ceiling, install recessed lighting or, with translucent plastic grids below fluorescent fixtures, create a "ceiling of light."

Beams. These are proving to be especially popular in traditional-styled kitchens, particularly those with colonial decor. They recall the old, stained wood beams, which were originally used as part of the house support. Today, simulated wood beams are made of lightweight plastic and easily installed.

A unique design for couples who cook, this kitchen is a modified U-shape arranged so two people can work in it easily. Mixing area for baking is at a lowered 32-inch height, surfaced with marble and butcher block. Two sinks are provided; all work areas are lighted by ceiling-mounted spots. Note these conveniences: tambour cabinet doors for spices and snack foods, open shelves near mixing and food-preparation areas, pull-out small-appliance cart, sit-down work area; work-saving appliances. *Courtesy General Electric.*

Excellent one-wall kitchen with all facilities close at hand. Double-bond stainless-steel sink is flanked by refrigerator and range areas; sink and trash compactor are built in under counter. Added touches include wall-installed microwave oven, vaulted wooden ceiling with beams, adjoining terrace. *Courtesy General Electric.*

White colonial cabinetry, blue countertops, red-and-blue matching wallcovering, windowshade and vinyl flooring contribute to a cozy feeling in this kitchen. Step-saving U-shape design promises best use of space and equipment as does the angled dining peninsula. Wicker chairs and lamp shade, cedar shingles and simulated wooden beams add decorative touches. *Courtesy Wood-Mode.*

Panels and tiles. They are often installed directly to a "dry wall" ceiling or wood furring strips, although, today, they can be used in a ceiling installation.

Most ceiling tiles available in plastic finishes serve as noise abaters but, if you particularly wish to deaden noise, it's a good idea to use acoustical tiles, which are designed to absorb sound.

Tiles come in a variety of textures and designs and in panels that lock together for a one-piece, solid look.

WINDOW TREATMENTS. A kitchen window with a view is lovely. If you have one, play it up by all means. Go ahead and be traditional—plan that sink in front of the window where you can gaze out on peace and tranquility. Or, put some other center there, such as the mixing or food preparation area.

If you don't have a view but want a window, fake one with any of the window treatments suggested.

But first, let's think a bit about windows.

Before you treat a window or "non-window," consider what you want that treatment to do:

1. To enjoy or camouflage a view?
2. To highlight a kitchen's decor?
3. To increase light or to help shade the sun?
4. To create privacy?

A window can solve almost any problem, depending on how you treat it.

SUGGESTIONS FOR WINDOW TREATMENTS

BLINDS	Wide selection of materials, styles and colors. Trim provides flexibility in styling. Control direct light. Provide privacy. Washable varieties for easy care.
WINDOW SHADES	Wide selection of materials, styles and colors. Do-it-yourself variety allows flexibility in adding trim, fringe or fabric to coordinate with wall covering or paint color. Same benefits as blinds, above.
CURTAINS	Wide selection of plain and fancy varieties. Cheerful, crisp, bright. Fabrics should be treated to withstand soil, grease, humidity. Cafe types are popular for kitchens.
SHUTTERS AND SCREENS	Many colors and finishes available. Easy to install. Provide privacy while maintaining light. Fold, slide open or remain stationary.
SKYLIGHTS	Excellent for natural daylight over work areas, eating centers. Conserve energy.
OTHER	Fake a window with any of the above solutions. Use a mural or wall covering to simulate an outdoor scene.

Modified U-shape kitchen displays a practical mix of wall cabinets, midway cabinets over sink and open shelves to left of refrigerator. Unique V-shape work island contains bar-sink, tray storage and telephone installation. *Courtesy General Electric.*

ACCESSORIES AND ACCESSORIZING. When the last knob has been put on the cabinets, the final kick plate installed, and all the appliances are plugged in or plumbed in and working, you're ready to accessorize.

This is fun time, the time in kitchen vernacular to "pour the syrup on the pancake" or "top the sundae with a cherry."

One of my pet beliefs is to have nothing in your kitchen that is merely beautiful. Your most treasured and attractive accessories are the tools of the trade—pots, pans, dinnerware, glassware, utensils and cookware.

Look behind your cabinet doors and inside the drawers. Chances are your prettiest accessories are waiting to burst forth into double-time duty.

Here is a suggested idea list to jog your thinking:

- Pots and pans.
- Copper and brass utensils.
- Wooden spoons, tools.
- Glass canisters filled with cooking ingredients—rice, pasta, flour, sugar, noodles, crackers, breadsticks, dried fruits.
- Herbs in pots and planters.
- Clock.

COLOR—AN IMPORTANT INGREDIENT. Long gone are the days when the kitchen was a white tile, sterile laboratory devoted to food preparation. Today, the kitchen has a multifaceted personality; it serves many functions for varied lifestyles. It has gone mod. It is wrapped in a rainbow of color. You've but to cast your eye about any 20th-century version to see major appliances, sinks, small appliances, countertops, flooring, wall covering, dinnerware, utensils and more, all sporting shades of gold, avocado, yellow, almond, red, blue, charcoal, browns, wood tones, persimmon; and they are coordinated to mix and match.

34

A multi-purpose, greenhouse-type window area highlights this "conservatory" kitchen with its clean, contemporary styling. Extended pass-through windows at the sink area make summer patio entertaining easy. Note microwave-oven center in an island arrangement. *Courtesy General Electric, William J. Ketcham CKD.*

Manufacturers of all these kitchen items have worked together to mix and match their wares for your selection in the marketplace. Pick almost any color and you'll find coordinates to match the smallest spatula, dishpan or wastebasket.

Even though it is easy to find a color scheme and your kitchen decor seems to fall together effortlessly, you should know some basics about color. The following tips will prove invaluable to you many times over as you begin to add the decorative touches to your new kitchen.

Get to know how colors work
- Yellow, red and orange create a "warm" atmosphere.
- Blues and greens create a "cool" feeling.
- Blacks, whites, grays, beiges are neutral and can be warm or cool, depending upon companion colors.
- Warm colors, such as orange or yellow, appear large.
- Cool colors, such as blue and green, appear small.
- You can add dimension or shrink space by the use of color.

Learn how to develop a color scheme
- Choose a predominant color. Use it in two-thirds of the kitchen. The walls, cabinetry or flooring are excellent choices to carry the leading color.
- Pick several coordinate colors that mix and match, or pick one companion color to set the mood.
- Consider patterns to add interest or to highlight the color scheme. An interesting wall covering, for example, can serve as the background of your color scheme, yet add dimension and character.
- Consider dimension. Textures, such as brick, stone and straw, are an excellent relief, add dimension and enhance color.

35

A kitchen styled for light. Recessed incandescent downlights are used here to light the front edge of the counter work surface. Supplementary under-cabinet fixtures light the back surface for uniformity. Local task areas (range top and sink) have additional fixtures located over each work plane. In the adjacent dining area (below) a decorative pendant fixture offers clear flame-shaped bulbs or low-wattage reflector bulbs in the downlight cylinders. *Courtesy Westinghouse.*

LIGHTING. Plan adequate general lighting and special lighting over counters, under wall cabinets and other strategic places.

Generally, you will need three types of lighting in every room of the house. They include *general illumination* which provides overall lighting throughout the room; *task lighting* for work centers; and *decorative lighting* for ambiance.

For kitchen lighting, you might consider fluorescent tubes. Their long, slender shape and cool operating temperatures are ideal. Select warm, white deluxe. The color is excellent and blends beautifully with incandescent lighting. The advantages of fluorescents are many: they produce three to four times as much light per watt as incandescents; keep the kitchen cooler; conserve energy; and last many times longer than most regular incandescents.

General illumination. Soft, general lighting helps to diffuse contrasts of brightness between work centers, cuts down on work shadows when supported by task lighting and supplies needed light inside cabinets. Ideas include:

- Ceiling-mounted or suspended fixtures.
- Fluorescent built-in lighting around the perimeter.
- Lighted beams.
- Luminous ceilings.

As a guide, for each 50 square feet of room, use 150 to 200 watts incandescent or 60 to 80 watts fluorescent.

Task lighting. Individual work areas should be well lighted in order to avoid working in your own shadow. One note of caution is that some sort of shield or shade for undercabinet or task lighting be provided to help avoid looking directly into the light.

Specially designed light fixture over island provides a wash of light while spot ceiling and undercounter fixtures supply task lighting. Planned storage behind sleek cabinetry is perfect for the homeowner who wants everything out of sight. Basic design is a broken-U with a work island. *Courtesy Wood-Mode.*

Decorative lighting. Use this to highlight areas, objects of art or other decorative items.

To help in your planning, refer to the chart below. Or, consult your local utility company who may have a kitchen planning or lighting department and may be able to offer you specific assistance. Also, your kitchen dealer or designer will be glad to assist you.

Kitchen Lighting Suggestions

Location	Type	Light Sources	Installation
Above sink	Fluorescent or Incandescent	**LOCAL LIGHTING** WWX tubes 75-watt reflector flood lights	Behind 8" faceboard or in recessed or surface-mounted fixture, well shielded. Spaced 15" apart in recessed high hats or surface mounted fixtures.
Above range With hood	Incandescent	60-watt soft white bulb min.	
With no hood	- - - - - - - - - - - - -	- - - - - - - - same as sink - - - -	- -
Above food preparation centers With cabinets above	Fluorescent	15-watt WWX 18" tube 20-watt WWX 24" tube 40-watt WWX 48" tube	Use longest tube that will fit and fill at least 2/3 of counter length. Install beneath cabinet attached to bottom of cabinet at front, or in fixture mounted at back wall; shielded.
No cabinets above	Incandescent	75-watt reflector flood lights or 100-watt standard bulb.	Space lights 32" apart over length of counter, either recessed downlights or surface mounted cylinders.
Above dining area Counter without cabinets above	Incandescent	75-watt reflector flood lights	See above.
Table & Chairs	Incandescent or Incandescent	150-watt or 50/150-watt 3-way soft white bulb. 40 or 60-watt soft white bulbs.	Single shade suspended fixture directing light up and down, 15" min. diameter shade; diffusing bowl or disc. Multiple arm suspended fixture, 18" min. spread, shielded.
Small kitchen (under 75 sq. ft.)	Incandescent or Fluorescent	**GENERAL LIGHTING** 150 watts min. 60 watts WWX, min.	Ceiling mounted or suspended; double number of fixtures when using recessed equipment.
Average kitchen (75-120 sq. ft.)	Incandescent or Fluorescent	150-200 watts total 60 to 80 watts WWX, min.	
Large kitchen (over 120 sq. ft.)	Incandescent or Fluorescent	2 watts/sq. ft. 3/4 watt to 1 watt/sq. ft.	

Courtesy General Electric Co.

4 | Plan for Work Centers

IT HAS BEEN said that any well-planned kitchen makes work easier and more satisfying, saves time, steps and energy, is easy to keep clean, eliminates confusion, is attractive, meets the needs of the family and encourages family cooperation. Well now, that's a big order, but not an impossible one to meet.

To accomplish all this, it is wise to follow a few basic planning principles that have been tried and proven by time and motion experts over the years. To do so will insure that you will eventually achieve the most efficient kitchen for your personal needs. What follows is a brief discussion of kitchen work centers and how they help to create a functional and workable kitchen. Once you've incorporated these basic work centers into an initial plan, the rest is up to you. Whatever design emerges will depend upon your personal tastes and your or your designer's creative genius.

APPLIANCE-BASED WORK CENTERS. Plan all your activities around three primary appliances—the dishwasher, the range and the refrigerator. They then become the *Clean-up* or *Sink/Dishwasher Center;* the *Cooking* or *Range Center;* and the *Food Preparation (Mixing and Baking)* or *Refrigerator Center.* Look at them individually. Analyze the activities that will take place there, and list all the utensils you will use there.

The clean-up or sink/dishwasher center. This is primarily the center of all kitchen activities and is used for the pre-preparation of foods and clean-up. It is located between the cooking and food preparation centers.

Also included in this area are the garbage disposer and/or trash compactor.

Consider these measurements
- Counter space—a minimum of 24 inches on each side of sink; 36 inches is better.
- Right-handed people work more efficiently if they have 36 inches of counter surface on the right for soiled items and foods to be prepared and 18 to 30 inches on the left for cleaned and prepared items. The reverse is true for the left-handed.

Store the following here
Dehydrated and canned soups
Dried beans, peas and fruits
Unrefrigerated fruits and vegetables
Coffee, tea, cocoa
Dishwashing and clean-up supplies

A clean-up center design that makes rare good sense. Dishwasher and trash compactor are installed at an angle for easy access. Twin-bowl, stainless-steel sink rounds out the practical plan. Dishwasher is an energy-saver model designed to heat its own water. *Courtesy Kitchen Aid.*

Cleansers
Double boiler
Measuring cups
Coffeepots and teapots
Paring knives
Glassware and dinnerware near dishwasher

Special tips

- Store items at point of first use, such as double boiler which needs water, measuring cups.
- Avoid a corner sink center, if possible. It takes up too much space, and the angle installation creates an obstacle in planning and working.
- Include a chopping block or ceramic counter inset, a pull-out cutting board or a portable cutting board for countertop or sink top.
- Allow 24 inches beside sink for dishwasher installation, now or later.

The cooking or range center. This area provides space for cooking and serving. The range you choose will determine how you use the space around it. For example, a built-in oven and cooktop installation requires an adequate working counter next to the oven, an item that is often overlooked. Also, such an installation reduces counter space, and so more working space should be provided in your planning.

A ventilation system is important for this area. This includes an exhaust fan and hood for removal of odor, grease, moisture and smoke.

Consider these measurements
- Counter space—24 inches on either side of range.
- Right-handed people need more counter space on the right and vice versa for left-handed workers.
- Include 24 inches of heatproof surface such as glass ceramic, stainless steel or ceramic tile, and a wood chopping block or counter inset for cutting.
- Built-in cooktop and oven installations reduce counter space by 42 to 48 inches. If the oven is installed away from cooking center, plan 24 inches of counter space next to or nearby it.
- A built-in cooktop is more efficient if working height is around 32 inches, although 36 is generally used.
- A built-in oven is more efficient if it is installed so the inside of the opened door is 5 to 7 inches below the elbow.

Large and functional work island in this kitchen contains built-in self-ventilating cooktop, and glass ceramic inset for pastry work. Oven cabinet contains conventional oven below and microwave above. Cabinetry is a contemporary design in grass green with laminated plastic-finished doors and drawers. *Courtesy Wood-Mode.*

Store the following near here
   Canned vegetables
   Fats and oils
   Seasonings and condiments
   Rice and pasta
   Cereals
   Instant coffee, tea, chocolate
   Bouillon
   Measuring cups and spoons

   Can opener
   Cooking tools
   Stirring spoons and forks
   Slotted spoons
   Serving bowls
   Cooking utensils
   Hand mixer
   Wire, cooling racks

Special tips
- Avoid placing the range next to the refrigerator. Both need counter space. Also, heat can affect the operation of the refrigerator when the refrigerator door is opened. If you cannot avoid such an installation, allow a minimum 3-inch space and provide some insulation if possible.
- Store small cooking appliances near this area and use them under the ventilating fan and hood.
- Adequate lighting is a must in the cooking area, as well as ample convenience outlets.

An easy-care range center with a self-cleaning oven/microwave oven combination teamed-up alongside built-in cooktop. A designer hood houses ventilating system for removal of cooking odors, fumes and grease. *Courtesy Thermador Tradewind.*

The food preparation or refrigerator center. Plan to do most of your food preparation in this area. Store the majority of your food items and food preparation utensils in this area. Allow ample storage for small electric appliances most often used in this area—hand mixer, standard mixer, blender, can opener, food processer, etc. The food preparation area is frequently combined with the range or cooking area, or is next to the refrigerator. How you plan the arrangement is dependent on the space available.

Consider these measurements
- Counter space—at least 36 to 42 inches. If the refrigerator is separated from the food preparation center, allow a minimum of 18 inches next to the latch side of the refrigerator or where the door swings open.
- Working height is most comfortable if the counter is 30 to 32 inches high, thus making it more efficient for rolling pastry, mixing, etc.

Store these in this area

Mixing bowls and spoons	Packaged mixes
Measuring cups and spoons	Shortenings, fats, oils
Rubber spatulas	Salad ingredients
Mixers and beaters	Freezer containers
Baking pans and sheets	Waxed paper
Rolling pins	Aluminum foil
Knives	Paper towels
Sifters	Plastic wraps
Refrigerator containers	Plastic bags
Flour	Bottle openers
Sugar	Pitchers
Spices and condiments	Ice-cream scoop
Baking ingredients	

Special tips
- Perforated hardboard attached to the wall is excellent for hanging small items, such as measuring spoons, spatulas, strainers, can openers, scissors, etc.
- Adequare lighting is a must here, as in any strategic working area; also, convenience outlets.
- A wood chopping block and special counter insets, such as glass ceramic or marble, for pastry and candy making, are helpful.

OTHER CENTERS

Eating. We seem to be spending more and more time in the kitchen as we opt for more casual living. Naturally, this calls for more gathering and dining space in the kitchen. Allot some space for a dining table and chairs or, if possible, you may wish to plan a more elaborate sitting/dining area in connection with the family room.

In this well-organized kitchen, the sink, food-preparation island, table and cooking center all form a step-saving triangle. Curtainless picture windows, allowing uncluttered view of countryside, are easy to clean. Pasta-themed wallcovering helps to define color scheme. *Courtesy General Tire.*

Consider these measurements

- A seated person extends about 20 inches from a table and requires about 32 inches for rising from the table.
- Allow 24 inches of table or counter space per person.
- For eating counters, plan a minimum depth of 15 inches if used only for breakfast or lunch; 24 inches if used for dinner.

Planning or desk area. You may find it convenient to plan a special area for menu planning, recipe writing, telephoning, storing recipes and cookbooks, planning community or church activities. A lowered counter of 30 inches is more comfortable for sitting, leaving space underneath for knees and provision for a drawer or file storage. If the counter is higher, a stool may be more comfortable. A wall phone with a long cord is excellent, because you can move the phone around with you while you work in the kitchen.

Laundry area. A laundry area is more ideally located in a utility room or another more convenient place apart from the kitchen. However, if you've no other location, it can be successfully combined with an adjacent kitchen area. Place it near the plumbing and separate it from the major food preparation areas either with a divider, an island or peninsula.

Pantry or storage center. Of course, you will plan adequate wall and base cabinet storage for each center. If possible, supplement this storage with a pantry area or storage wall. Include utility cabinets with pull-out shelves and wall and base cabinets with counter space. Use it for small appliances, large, infrequently used utensils, items for entertaining, linen.

And: Don't forget to consider centers for other activities, such as sewing, flower arranging, herb growing.

5 | Cabinets and Countertops

STORAGE EFFICIENCY is the mainstay of a good kitchen. In a kitchen, as anywhere else in the house, you literally need a place for everything. Perhaps even more so in a kitchen. Besides being so obvious, disorder in a kitchen can become a decided obstacle to working efficiency.

Cabinet selection, ample storage and arrangement of work centers combine to create order in a kitchen.

Before you select cabinetry, it is important that you determine how you will use your kitchen and what your daily and special storage needs are. That's why we carefully outlined the principles of center planning, in Chapter 4, and listed the items that should be stored in specific work centers.

Plan where you will store everything, right down to the last salt and pepper shaker. Make sure you have ample storage for small appliances. Consider the convenience of cabinet organizers, special-purpose units and accessories that automatically organize kitchen storage and save work, space, stooping, stretching and kitchen clutter.

To Determine How Much Storage Is Needed
- Allow 6 square feet of shelf space for each person.
- Plan for an additional 12 square feet if you entertain frequently.
- Increase storage according to the things you plan to acquire.

CABINETS. There are several ways to acquire cabinets. They can be built-on-site, by a professional carpenter; ordered from a stock or standard line; or custom-built. Or you can build them yourself.

Built-on-site cabinets installed on the spot provide storage. They often lack standards of construction and quality control, and there is more chance for error. A fineness of detail and quality may be lacking, depending upon who builds them. Unless you have complete confidence in the carpenter, or draw up your own specifications, supervising each step of the way, you have no guarantee of satisfaction. But, if you are so inclined, it can be done.

Step-by-step directions for building your own cabinets are given in Part II.

Stock or standard line cabinets are ready-made and may be ordered. They cost less than those which are custom-made, and while they provide certain specialized conveniences, they must be adjusted to fit your kitchen requirements. When stock cabinets do not fit the plan exactly, fillers are used to "fill out" the space. Look for the certification seal of the National Kitchen Cabinet Association which assures you that the cabinets meet certain standards of quality, including structural testing, finishes and laboratory tests to determine durability under stress. Ask about them.

Kitchen cabinets and bath vanities that bear this National Kitchen Cabinet Association certification seal have been tested to assure years of service despite hard use. The cabinet finish must be able to resist food and grease stains to win NKCA certification.

If you have specialized requirements or want a kitchen made just to your specifications, you may have to choose cabinets which are custom-made. You can have them in custom-treated, standard-sized units or have them built to your own personal needs—base cabinet higher or lower to suit your height, storage cabinets designed for over- or undersized items—whatever the need. Count on six to eight weeks delivery, or longer if you have an unusually special order.

You may choose between wood and metal cabinets, metal cabinets with wood fronts or plastic laminates.

Styles vary among colonial, traditional, contemporary, provincial and Mediterranean.

Here are their characteristics.

TYPE	CHARACTERISTICS
WOOD	Durable.
	Can be built to suit any specification.
	Easy-care stain finish; scratches can be touched-up.
	Soft woods—pine, fir, knotty pine, knotty cedar, hemlock.
	Hard woods—birch, oak, maple, walnut, cherry, pecan, beech, alder, ash, Philippine mahogany, teak, sandalwood.
	Warpage may be controlled with adequate air-conditioning system and humidity control.
METAL	Extremely durable.
	Some finishes may be scratch resistant; painted ones may scratch easily; harder to touch up.
	May be repainted.
	Choice of exciting colors.
	Cabinets available with wood doors in changeable panels—plastic, fabric, grillwork.
PLASTIC	Many types: Melamine, polyester laminates. Plasticized vinyls. Molded urethanes.
	High-pressure laminates made of several sheets of heavy kraft paper; top sheet printed with desired pattern, such as wood grain; thinner, less expensive, but durable; usually 1/16″ thick (same as countertops); also 1/32″.
	May chip under heavy wear or abuse.
	Heat resistant; not fireproof.

Refrigerator and freezer fronts are paneled to match these handsome ash cabinets with toned ceramic pulls. Note pull-up cutting board at end of island. Hidden storage conveniences include roto and lazy-susan shelves, slide-out vegetable bins and cuttng boards, waste receptacle, cutlery drawer divider, metal breadbox and in-cabinet lighting. *Courtesy Haas.*

A mix of white cabinetry and color touches on soffit, counters and flooring give this kitchen a light and cheerful theme. Large range hood provides a symmetrical balance for the cooking island. Lowered counter with knee opening is ideal for mixing, food preparation or planning. *Courtesy Wood-Mode.*

A kitchen with a concept. Total storage is provided through the use of utility cabinets with adjustable shelves. Every cabinet faces large center island which houses cooking and clean-up facilities as well as storage and counter space for food preparation. From left to right (below), cabinets reveal dinnerware, utility supplies, utensils, non-refrigerated fruits, vegetables and cereals, slide out storage for pots, pans and linens, small appliances, canned goods, bar unit with sink and glassware, wine rack, desk unit and books shelves. *Courtesy Mutschler.*

V-joint cabinetry in oak with a country finish is just right for this kitchen in a colonial home. Country finish is repeated in ventilating hood mounted on the brick wall, originally the exterior brick wall of the house and retained in a previous add-on remodeling. Large center island helps this large and open kitchen maintain the efficiency of a smaller one and direct traffic flow away from work area. *Courtesy Wood-Mode.*

Here's ample storage, readily accessible, special-purpose units contain pull-to-you base cabinets, waste basket and specially designed canned goods pantry. Unusually engineered work island is divided by a raised panel ledge and separates cooktop, grilling and oven. Kitchen is adjoined by a pass-through counter to family room. *Courtesy Wood-Mode.*

Elegance and warmth are created by cabinetry of solid oak slats, stained in black, enhanced with silver-colored edges and hardware. Complementary smoked-glass-framed cabinetry and doors show off dinner and glassware. Interior built-in fittings, dining area and unique arched window make this a dream kitchen for all seasons. *Courtesy Poggenpohl.*

When selecting cabinetry . . .

1. In any given area, select the widest cabinet possible. The space is more useful, and the cabinet more economical.
2. Standard cabinet sizes are 9 to 48 inches wide in 3-inch increments. Base cabinets are 34½ inches high, 24 inches deep. Wall cabinets are 30 to 33 inches high, 12 inches deep.
3. Check hinges for ease of convenience and safety.
4. Look for adjustable shelves.

With acquisition of today's unique and upbeat cabinetry styling, it is possible to build in many specialized storage features. Utilizing these special-purpose designs will increase your storage efficiency and kitchen organization.

Some of these specially designed cabinets may be standard, but most are optional choices, so plan to pay extra for them.

PLANNED STORAGE.

If you have specialized storage needs or if you simply wish to organize your kitchen conveniently, you're sure to find just the cabinet or drawer you're looking for in this section. Some of these conveniences are standard in any cabinet line; others are optional. Most cabinet manufacturers offer units similar to those shown here. Ask your kitchen specialist about them.

Versatile and sturdy pull-out counter can also serve as a lowered work counter for mixing and food preparation.

Built-in wine rack assures proper positioning for bottles in lattice-work slots.

Special shelf pops up mixer at just the right height and keeps it out of sight when unused.

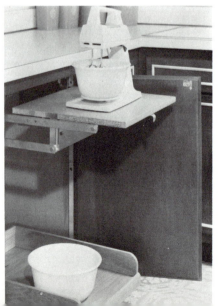

Divided cutlery drawer and a metal-lined bread box are handy organizational musts.

A pull-out serving cart with two shelves and an expandable top with two 6″ drop leaves.

A pantry storage cabinet with full-width shelf and lazy-susan at top, pull-out trays and drawers beneath.

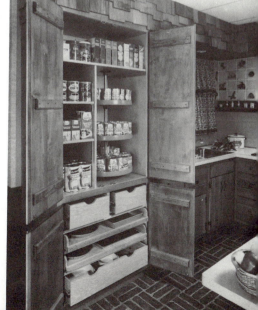

All photos courtesy Wood-Mode

Pull-out one-can-depth base cabinet pantry storage is really convenient for often-used items.

Dinnerware cabinet with variable-designed adjustable shelving and cup rack; silverware drainer with tarnish-proof lining.

Pull-out wooden dining table for super-compact areas. *All photos Coppes Napanee.*

Cabinet with utility pull-out for cleaning items, convenient for organization in clean-up center (left) Drawers for pots and pans avoid cabinet clutter (right).

Storage cabinet with ventilated bins are perfect for produce. *All photos courtesy Tielsa.*

Close-up of wall and base cabinet installation shows efficient use of space with open-shelf pocket slots and canister bins.

Cutaway cross-section shows a variety of super fittings for cabinet organization. Left to right, pull-out basket under-range drawer, utility drawer, corner susan with wire racks, bread slicer with bread storage cabinet, drainer racks, slide-out rack, pull-out cutting board, bottle cabinet, utility storage and canister/vegetable utility cabinet. *Photos courtesy Allmilmo.*

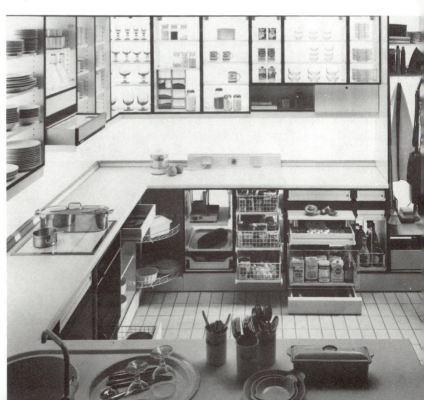

Foods are both visible and accessible in pull-out wire baskets in this storage cabinet.

Storage cabinet with specialized fittings permits foodstuffs to be organized for maximum visibility. *Photos courtesy Allmilmo.*

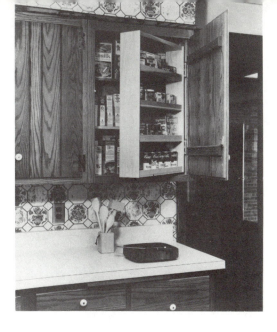

Swing-out wall-cabinet spice rack allows access to adjustable shelves.

Food file, today's version of an old-fashioned pantry, permits easier access than its 18-inch width would indicate.

Tray storage is provided under a drawer in this 12-inch base cabinet. *Photos courtesy Rutt Custom Kitchens.*

Tambour door cabinet camouflages small-appliance storage.

Blind corner susan provides accessible pot and pan storage.

A base cabinet food file makes rare good sense when it offers hinged shelving to allow better use of space. *Photos courtesy Rutt Custom Kitchens.*

Cabinet with swing-out storage and adjustable shelves help you find items at a glance.

Pull-out waste basket is removable to ease trash disposal.

Pull-out 1½-inch-thick maple block provides comfortable surface for chopping, mincing.

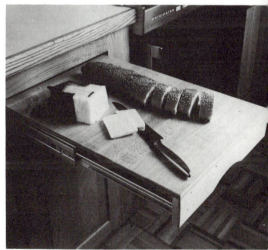

Photos courtesy Crystal Cabinet Works.

COUNTERTOPS. Kitchen counters provide the framework for your kitchen plan. Besides their practical role as a work surface, they offer a major contribution to overall decor.

Which of your kitchen work centers will require specilized surfaces? Do you need a heat-resistant surface near the cooking area? A wood chopping block next to the food preparation center? A glass ceramic or marble surface for bread, pastry and candy-making?

Is the counter you are considering durable, resistant to heat, stain and spotting, and is it easy to care for?

Which material should you choose? The most popular are plastic laminate and ceramic tile for overall surfaces. Insets for specialized work centers include wood, glass ceramic and stainless steel.

Overall countertop surfaces

Laminated plastic. This is a high-pressure laminate, usually 1/16 inch thick. It is easy to maintain, heat and stain resistant, but not recommended for cutting and chopping. The design may be *self-edge,* which is flat with the edge of the same material and a separate 4-inch backsplash, or it may be *post-formed,* an all-in-one unit with a curved sweep from the bottom of the front edge to the top of the backsplash.

Ceramic tile. This is either glazed or quarry tile. It withstands heat and is available in a variety of designs, sizes and color combinations. Its hard surface encourages dish and utensil breakage.

Solid plastic. This has the appearance of marble and is heat and stain resistant. It can be sawed and cut just like wood.

Counter insets

Hardwood. This is either natural or laminated and recommended for food preparation areas or cutting surfaces. It is not heatproof.

Glass ceramic. This is heat resistant, ideal for kneading or slicing, smooth, stain resistant and easy to maintain. It is excellent near range or cooking surfaces.

Marble. This has the same characteristics and uses as glass ceramic, but is not as durable. It stains easily and shows scratches.

Stainless steel. This is sturdy and heat resistant. It scratches easily, though it quickly gains a natural patina with use. It also water spots, but cleans easily.

6 | Appliances

A KITCHEN is as efficient as its appliances are convenient. The appliances are responsible for the cooking, dishwashing, refrigerating, freezing, garbage and trash disposal. Convenience features on these appliances, designed to meet your needs, are what help to make your work easier.

Decide early on what appliances you plan to keep and which ones you wish to replace or add to your kitchen.

If you are remodeling in stages, plan for future installations now. Install a 24-inch base cabinet, for example, which will be replaced eventually by a dishwasher, or a 15-inch base cabinet where you plan to put in a compactor. In the first stage install needed utility and drain connections for water, gas and electricity.

BUILT-INS. "Shall we install built-ins or not?" "What are the installation problems involved with built-ins?" These are frequently asked questions. Built-ins provide a certain sophisticated look to a new kitchen, but you should know there are trade-offs. They may utilize more space, for one thing. A built-in oven and cooktop, as we said earlier, will require more space than a freestanding range. But high on their list of favorable aspects is flexibility, in that you can install them in separate areas. They don't have to be placed together. Also, keep in mind that most appliances have a "thin-line" look, and once installed, look built in. This is, of course, more economical than opting for true built-ins.

You might also consider the following appliances.

Refrigerator/freezer combination.

Freezer.

Dishwasher.

Laundry equipment.

Keep-warm oven.

Barbecue grill and griddle.

Built-in can opener.

Built-in toaster.

Built-in paper and wrap dispenser.

Note: Refrigerators and freezers may be installed side by side, on top of each other in models designed for that purpose or placed separately in the kitchen. Plan on a clearance of 3 inches all around for air circulation.

SELECTING AND SHOPPING FOR NEW APPLIANCES. Evaluate each appliance you plan to include in the new kitchen, following the check list below. Study it carefully before you make a final purchase. Selecting features that are especially suited to your needs and your particular set of circumstances will prove most useful and convenient. Why do you need it? This should be your first consideration.

Budget. Life-cycle costs, operating costs, anticipated service and service contracts.

Space availability. Size, clearance requirements, clearance entries prior to installation.

Capacity or size. Family and individual lifestyle requirements.

Safety features and certification seals. The American Gas Association Blue Star Seal for safety, durability and performance; the UL (Underwriters Laboratories) Safety Seal on electrical appliances tested for fire, electrical shock and related hazards; the Association of Home Appliances Certification Seal for key performance or capacity characteristics of refrigerators and freezers, air conditioners, dehumidifiers and others as announced.

Special convenience features. Make certain you need each feature and will use it. As features increase, cost increases.

New innovations. If you are purchasing a totally new innovation—a departure from a conventional design—ask about operation and performance results in relation to your expectation. Give yourself time to get used to a new method.

Quality construction. Consider demands that will be made on the appliance: easy-to-clean features, durable finishes and materials, drawers that slide out easily, doors that close firmly, shelves that are sturdy. Look for sharp or rough edges.

Color and style. Decide on your decor before purchasing appliances. Will the color chosen adapt to future decorating plans?

Cost of delivery and installation. These may be hidden costs unless you ask *before* the sale.

Dealer and/or servicing agency. Does dealer service appliances? If not, who is the authorized servicer?

Examine the product. Take time; ask questions; ask for a demonstration; ask neighbors and friends about their experiences; ask to see a use and care manual *before* you make a decision, to help you ask pertinent questions.

Energy-saving features. Look for any special energy-saving features. (See Chapter 10.)

Price in relation to convenience and service. As features and convenience increase, prices increase accordingly. Economy models should perform basic functions and be durable.

Warranty. What are the terms? What is expected of the manufacturer? The buyer? The dealer? Service agency? Make certain you study and understand all warranty provisions *before* purchase.

When shopping for your new appliances, shop very carefully. We cannot urge you enough to do your homework. Arm yourself with the facts, list pertinent questions in advance that you want to ask the dealer or salesperson.

To help you focus more clearly on available features and important buying considerations, study the information below. Develop your own guidelines to informed decision-making.

RANGES. Select a gas or electric model, depending upon installation requirements, personal preferences, availability and cost. Generally, the same features are available on both. However, some buyers opt for the instantaneous shut-off capability of heat in a gas range, while others prefer the retained heat capacity of electric units.

Electric ranges usually require a 220/240 volt line. Some metropolitan areas require a lower voltage, and it is wise to inquire about voltage requirements at point of purchase or from a local, qualified electrician. Gas ranges require a 115-volt circuit for lights, controls and a gas supply line.

You'll find a wide variety of models from a vast selection of types and designs. Choose from: *freestanding designs* with one or two ovens and broilers; *eye-level models* featuring an oven above the surface units or burners and one oven below; *built-in surface cooktops;* individual *built-in single* or *double ovens; freestanding slide-in* and *drop-in models* to be set in between cabinets for a built-in look; and *stack-on* types for countertop or special base-cabinet installation. Your choice depends upon personal preference and space availability.

Special cabinetry is available for built-in ovens. Some may be stacked onto a base cabinet or counter, or they may be available with a special wraparound cover or installed flush with or into a wall. Look for a variety of designs in built-in ovens—a single oven, oven and warmer, two ovens in a single frame or an oven and separate broiler.

Installation. Cooktops may be installed directly into the countertop and, depending upon the number of units or burners, will fit into cabinets from 15 to 48 inches wide or larger. Installation is flexible. They may be installed in a peninsula or in an island instead of in a cabinet. The area below may be enclosed for storage or it may be left open, depending upon preference. Your personal height is important, however, in the ultimate decision on where and how your range top should be installed. If you are less than 5 feet, 4 inches tall, range tops may be installed at a height of 32 inches. Those of average height will find that a height of 36 inches is comfortable. If you're taller than average, you may find that it is necessary to raise the height of your range top, through a specially elevated installation.

Built-in ovens should be installed according to your height and work preferences. An oven installation with the oven door between 5 and 7 inches below the elbow when open is convenient.

Convenience features. Convenience features abound in today's ranges. You'll find oven timers, clocks that turn ovens on and off automatically, automatic meat thermometers, rotisseries, warming shelves, grills, thermostatically controlled burners and units, cook and hold settings, speed broilers, infrared gas broilers, signal lights, infinite heat controls, changeable decorative door panels and self-ventilating ranges and built-ins.

Both freestanding and built-in ovens and ranges have been designed with current and up-to-date conveniences. A cooktop, for example, may come in a wide range of sizes and types. Many have temperature-controlled burners or units. Controls may be on the front panel or on the cooktop. Your choice will depend upon your work habits, safety considerations (one with controls on the cooktop rather than on the front panels, away from the reach of small children) or kitchen design requirements.

In addition to the regular gas or electric units or burners, cooktops may be smooth ceramic or glass, and available on freestanding ranges as well. Some utilize induction heat with the heat source located under the cooking surface.

Perhaps the most outstanding convenience feature available today is automatic oven-cleaning. This is available in two choices—self-cleaning and continuous-cleaning. In a self-cleaning oven, the soil is cleaned during a separate high-heat cycle. With continuous-cleaning models, oven surfaces are specially treated to clean during the cooking operation. The latter has not proved to be as effective as the automatic self-cleaning type, but if you don't mind a few stains, you may find it suitable for your purposes. It is less expensive initially and in operating costs. However, the self-cleaning feature, which costs more, is minimal in operating costs and energy consumption, because the oven retains heat more effectively, due to the thicker insulation necessary for the self-cleaning operation.

Innovations. The newest range innovation is the *convection* oven, which utilizes forced-air heat distribution. Convection cooking is said to be faster than a conventional oven, but not as fast as a microwave oven. It is most like the traditional radiant-heat oven, but the convection oven differs in that it is equipped with a fan that blows the heated air over the food and thereby cooks it faster at lower temperatures.

Induction cooking, mentioned above in connection with smooth ceramic or glass surfaces, is a magnetic process. Magnetic coils beneath the cooking surface produce a magnetic field, and when a stainless steel pan is placed on the unit, it attracts the field and produces heat, heating only the surface underneath the pan.

Microwave or electronic ovens, though available for some time now, are still relatively new on the market. A microwave oven cooks with microwaves or radio waves. A magnetron tube produces high-frequency waves that bombard the food and excite the molecules within the food-producing heat. Paper or glass utensils and pans, designed exclusively for microwave ovens, must be used. This oven offers the convenience of quick cooking and is ideal for today's fast-paced lifestyle. It is available as a built-in, table or countertop, freestanding or eye-level, or in a combination model. Some models require 220/240 volt installation; others 110 or 115 volts, in which case cooking time is longer.

Note: It should be pointed out that with any new innovation on the market, whether it be an appliance or an automobile, it is wise to familiarize yourself with its features and give yourself time to adjust to new methods and procedures. You may find this particularly true with smooth-surface ranges, microwave ovens, convection ovens and continuous-cleaning ranges, because their methods of operation are different from the conventional types you are familiar with and your expectations may differ from the actual performance.

REFRIGERATOR/FREEZERS. Select from one of two types—the combination refrigerator/freezer with two separate doors or a conventional one-door model with an inside frozen-food storage compartment. The combinations are designed with the freezer on top, bottom or with two sections side by side.

The freezer section in a conventional one-door refrigerator is used only for making ice cubes and very short-time storage of commercially frozen foods. It maintains temperatures from 10 to 15° F.

In the combination two-door model, the freezer is more than a compartment or a freezer section. It is an actual freezer maintaining temperatures from –5° F to +5° F. Some are fully automatic, no-frost models; others have to be defrosted manually.

The frostless models, which defrost automatically, offer the consumer increased convenience, but increases running time and, hence, operating costs. Their noise level is also higher. If you wish to determine how much a new refrigerator or freezer will cost to operate, check the energy consumption figures; then, to compute the average operating cost, multiply the KWH (kilowatt hours per month) figure by the energy cost on your electric bill. By now, you may be finding new labels on many major appliances containing energy information. This will offer you the opportunity to consider energy cost in each purchase decision where the information is available. (See Chapter 10, Design an Energy-Efficient Kitchen, for further discussion about appliance labeling and the Federal Trade Commission ruling.)

Convenience features. Look for the many new convenience features, which include: adjustable shelves; removable parts for easy maintenance; special storage compartments for meats, vegetables, fruit, eggs and dairy products; exterior dispensers for chilled water, ice and fruit juice; automatic ice makers; add-on ice makers; powersaver switches for reduction of power consumption and operating costs; lighted interiors; casters or rollers; and special decorative panels.

Other important considerations. Consider *size* carefully in your model choice. Models are available from compact designs to very large family-size units. Chances are you can find just the right size to fit the space available, though size should be based upon individual needs. Fresh food storage compartments should be approximately 8 cubic feet for a family of two and 1 cubic foot for each additional person. Add 2 cubic feet, if you entertain a great deal. The freezer space should supply about 2 cubic feet per person.

It is wise to check the required kitchen and ventilation space, door and hallway clearance for delivery and whether the installation requires a right- or left-hand door opening. Some models may have reversible doors.

FREEZERS. Choose from two types—the upright design and the chest type. To determine size and provided you have ample space, plan on allowing about 6 cubic feet per family member.

Upright freezers. This type utilizes less floor space. You'll find it much easier to place packages for freezing or to retrieve them for use. Defrosting methods are the same as those for refrigerator/freezers—manual and self-defrosting. Sizes are similar to refrigerators.

Chest freezers. This type requires more floor space than uprights—the larger, the more space. It is often easier to store the more bulky packages in a chest type, because of the depth and fewer shelves. Some chest models have specially designed countertops and, when installed at the end of a counter, will supply additional work space. Inasmuch as the lid lifts upward, it is wise to account for the height of this opening, if you wish to install cabinetry above. Large chest-type freezers are generally located in areas other than the kitchen, unless, of course, there is ample room along one wall. Sizes range from approximately 32 to 72 inches wide by 27 to 32 inches deep and 36 inches high.

Compact designs are available in both chest and upright models.

Convenience features. Door lock; signal light to indicate whether current is on or off or temperature too high; automatic reset mechanism or motor protection device; adequate drain for easy water removal on no-frost models; removable basket for adjustable shelves; counterbalanced lid on chest freezers; certification of refrigerated volume and shelf space on upright models, and refrigerated volume on chest models, which will provide accurate comparison among brands and with your old model; separate quick-freeze section; well-lighted interior; easy-to-read and accessible controls; rollers or casters for mobility in cleaning; energy-saving devices.

It is always important to inquire as to whether or not the warranty provides for food loss, and if so, in what amount and under what conditions.

DISHWASHERS. You'll find models which are freestanding, built-in, portable and convertible. The convertible can be used as a portable initially, then built-in permanently later. Space-savers include undersink types and a combination eye-level range and dishwasher. In the combination, the dishwasher is where a bottom oven would normally be.

Convenience features. Features include: flexible racks for easy loading; booster units to raise water temperature (if necessary); energy-saving devices; special cycles for short wash, rinse and hold, pre-rinse, pots and pans, gentle, soak; more than one wash cycle; automatic detergent and rinse agent dispensers;

convenient cord length and cord storage for portable and convertible models; handle and casters on portable units for easy mobility; stop switch; cycle indicator; spray arms and impellers for water distribution; rust- and scratch-resistant tub and door linings; cutting-board tops on free-standing units.

GARBAGE DISPOSERS

Types. Look for two types—batch-feed and continuous-feed models.

The batch-feed design is activated by the cover, which is set in place after the disposer is filled and ready for grinding. The cover is locked into position, whereupon the grinder is activated and the unit disposes of one "batch" at a time. There is a safety element built into this type in that the unit is not activated until the cover is in position.

The continuous-feed model is activated by a wall switch. This on-off switch allows you to add waste "continuously" while the disposer is operating. A rubber backsplash, fitted into the opening, helps to keep waste and water in place.

Installation requirements. There may be local ordinances which prohibit the use of a disposer. Check with your plumber or an authorized agent to determine the legality of its use. Make certain your sewage system is adequate to handle such residue. Inquire, too, about acoustical installation for sound control. Generally, the installation of a batch-feed unit is less costly than a continuous-feed design, even though it is more expensive initially. Installation costs are reduced if you install both the dishwasher and disposer at the same time.

Disposer and septic tank. If the septic tank is properly designed and is of adequate size for your home and family, you may use a disposer with the septic tank system. Check the current FHA Minimum Property Standards for septic tanks. Regulations for disposers, dishwashers and washing machines require:

Capacity	House Size (Number of Bedrooms)
• 750-gallon tank	2-bedroom house
• 900 gallon tank	3-bedroom house
• 1,000-gallon tank	4-bedroom house

Convenience features. Features include: a heavy-duty motor; high-bulk cutters for husks, corncobs; grind wheel and shredder rings; insulating material to minimize noise; corrosion-resistant parts; anti-jamming features; a circuit breaker or automatic switch to prevent overheating of motor or an overload reset to prevent overloading.

Plumbing. If you are planning to include a dishwasher or garbage disposer in your new plans, be sure to have a plumbing contractor check the waste line to make certain it will accommodate the appliances and that the installation meets building codes. If there is a septic tank, this should also be checked for adequacy.

Kitchen laundry installations should be placed as near to the plumbing facilities as possible. Also, locate water heaters and water-softener systems as close to point of use as possible so as to avoid long pipe runs.

Don't sacrifice good planning just to keep insufficient plumbing.

TRASH COMPACTORS. Models include freestanding and undercounter designs. One of the newest innovations to hit the kitchen design scene, trash compactors will compress trash to one quarter its original volume. It will crush most waste, including glass, metal cans, plastic bottles and cartons. It should be pointed out that it does not replace the garbage disposer. It does its best work on dry trash.

Features. A trash compactor measures from 15 to 18 inches, utilizes a 115-volt circuit and operates with a ⅓-horsepower motor. Trash is compressed into self-contained packages which weigh about 20 to 25 pounds. Water-resistant, polyethylene-lined kraft bags fit inside the unit to hold trash until it is ready for compaction, disposition and pickup.

WATER HEATERS. Look for gas or electric models. Selection is dependent upon your preference and/or availability of fuel supply. Gas models require a gas supply line, and electric designs a 220/240-volt circuit. Both gas and electric models are available in quick-recovery and standard-storage designs. Quick-recovery heaters are equipped with super-quick heaters, thus increasing their heating capacity over standard-storage models. It might pay, depending upon location of the heater and use, to consider a smaller capacity, quick-recovery type over a larger storage-type model. Discuss the pros and cons with your water-heater dealer.

Size. In making a decision about size, take into consideration family size and hot-water needs. For example, the number of showers and baths taken, how much laundering is done and the number of appliances in the home that utilize hot water. Capacity sizes range from 30 gallons to 100 gallons.

It is also important to consider future needs for hot water as lifestyles change. You may obtain sizing recommendations from the Gas Appliance Manufacturers Association, 1901 North Fort Meyer Drive, Suite 900, Arlington, Virginia 22209.

Gas water heaters should carry certification of performance and/or durability and safety.

Installation requirements. If your present water-heater capacity is small and you are planning to add a dishwasher for the first time or even a compact washing machine, consider the installation of a supplemental water heater in the kitchen. This may be installed under the counter or in a corner. Even though water heaters are not often included in kitchen installations, a small unit may just fit in perfectly in an otherwise wasted corner.

In planning the proper location for a water heater, consider the provision of an easily accessible drain valve. It is important for the drainage of accumulated mineral deposits. This can be especially true in hard-water areas. Though such deposits rarely decrease heating efficiency or affect the tank itself, they can effect a minor reduction in storage capacity.

Locate gas water heaters as close as possible to a vertical vent for drawing out combustion products and providing adequate air circulation.

SINKS. You'll find models available in porcelain enamel on cast iron, which comes in many colors and styles, and in stainless steel. A combination of chrome and nickel components makes stainless-steel sinks corrosion-resistant.

Sinks come with one, two or three bowls. Some are designed for a corner. Most have center compartments for installing a disposer.

Note: If you select a two-bowl type, consider having one bowl deeper than the other. If you have a dishwasher, one bowl may be adequate. You will have more flexibility, however, with two bowls.

Faucet assemblies include single-levers with a water mixer for desired temperature and two-faucet combinations.

Convenience features. The most often desired features include hardwood cutting board tops; retractable rinse-sprays; removable control drains; built-in food centers; soap and lotion dispensers; attachments for purification.

VENTILATING SYSTEMS. According to the Home Ventilating Institute, the kitchen which gets down to the business of serious cooking could produce over 200 pounds each year of grease-laden moisture in the average home. Odor, grease, smoke, excess heat and moisture are all natural by-products of cooking.

A well-planned kitchen should include a range hood and fan or blower, or a wall or ceiling exhaust fan to remove cooking by-products.

Ventilating systems include the ducted type—a range hood and blower or fan—installed to discharge air through an outside wall or one of the ductless types, which includes a hood and fan and utilizes a built-in filtering system that circulates air through replaceable filters. They remove odor, smoke and grease, but not heat.

The best system is a hood and blower which ducts to the outdoors. If ducting is out of the question and you've no other method of ventilation, your best bet, then, is a ductless ventilating hood and fan.

Points to keep in mind
- All range hoods and wall and ceiling exhaust fans bearing the Home Ventilation Institute (HVI) seal are certified for their capacity to move air and for sound level.
- Hood performance is measured in CFM (Cubic Feet per Minute). This is the volume of air the fan or blower removes each minute it operates. Air in kitchens should change about every four minutes.
- The best system should have an air removal capacity of 300 CFM to 400 CFM and exhaust up to 85 to 90 percent of all cooking fumes.
- To determine the best system for you, multiply the number of square feet of the kitchen floor by two. For example, 150 square feet would require a fan with 300 CFM rating. High-ceilinged rooms require a higher CFM rating.
- Check to see if local building codes set minimum CFM ratings. The Home Ventilating Institute and the Federal Housing Administration require a fan that will deliver a minimum of 40 CFM per foot of hood length.

A counter and backsplash wall of ceramic tile add the assurance of easy-care maintenance to this recessed cooking niche. Heavy-duty vent-hood and fan will remove fumes, cooking odors and grease. Warming shelf is a convenient feature. *Courtesy Thermador Tradewind.*

A cooking niche with a custom-designed, heavy-duty ventilating system. Note contrasting tiled insets, cooktop and center grill, plate rail and tiled wall. *Courtesy Thermador Tradewind.*

Large ceiling beams and massive uprights create a handsome framework for the butcher-block work table and counter with built-in cooktop. Over the smooth-surface cooktop and barbecue grill is a range hood of slate banded with wood that complements oak cabinetry. White porcelain knobs, checkered wallcovering and vinyl brick flooring complete the traditional look. *Courtesy Wood-Mode.*

A free-standing range does its best work when it is ventilated adequately. This attractive, specially mounted hood contains fan and blower assembly ducted for removal of cooking wastes. Wallcovering is washable and wipeable. *Courtesy Broan.*

Installation requirements*

Under cabinet. The hood is simply screwed to the bottom of the cabinet.

Wall hung. Most manufacturers provide special mounting brackets to make installation simple when there are no cabinets.

Ducting. Most hoods offer two-way discharge, horizontal or vertical through a standard 3¼″ x 10″ duct. In either case, the height of the hood over the cooking surface is important. 21″ to 24″ is recommended. 30″ is maximum.

Duct runs

1. *Outside wall.* If your range is located on an exterior wall, duct horizontally through the wall. This is the most economical installation and also gives top performance, because the duct run is so short it offers practically no resistance.

2. *Through attic to roof or eave.* This is usually the most efficient and economical installation, if the range is located on an inside wall and there is attic space above.

3. *Through soffit to outside wall.* This is often the best solution when the range is located on an inside wall in a two-story house.

4. *Between joists to outside wall or eave.*

5. *When "there's no way"—under ceiling to outside wall.* Suppose you can't use (2) because you have a two-story house. You can't use (3) because you have no soffit or don't want to take the old one out. You can't use (4) because the joists run the wrong way or you don't want to tear up your ceiling.

*Courtesy of Broan Manufacturing.

There's still a way to duct outside if you want good kitchen ventilation.

Attach the duct under the ceiling and cover it with a false wood beam or, perhaps, you can think of a better way to camouflage it.

Remember: Don't use a duct smaller than 3¼" x 10" rectangular or 6" round. (High-capacity hoods for indoor barbecues require larger duct sizes. Follow manufacturer's recommendations.)

If you have a choice of several duct runs, the shortest and straightest is the most efficient. (A 90° elbow is equal to about 10 feet of duct.)

Use roof jacks and wall caps that are designed for use with kitchen ventilators. These are designed to handle adequate flow of air and most have built-in dampers to prevent cold drafts.

HEATING AND COOLING. Generally, more thought is given to heating and cooling other areas of the house, but there are certain important considerations to keep in mind for kitchen installations.

Heating. Forced hot-water heating systems utilize "baseboard" heating panels in ceiling installations to relinquish floor space.

Consider installing forced warm-air registers into walls, if floor system is not practical.

Radiators using steam or hot-water systems can be concealed behind perforated metal frames, provided this does not reduce heating capacity. Installation is best on an outside wall or near a window.

Cooling. Consider the installation of a room air conditioner in or near your kitchen, if you do not have central air conditioning with a thermostat. An air conditioner can be a boon on those days when cooking is heavy and the weather hot. Make certain, however, you have an air conditioner of proper capacity. Consult an air conditioner dealer, your kitchen designer or dealer, a utility company or an electrician.

7 | Kitchen Utilities

BEHIND THE scenes, a kitchen is comprised of important utilities that make it run smoothly. In addition to those elements we have already discussed—plumbing, ventilation, lighting, storage, cabinetry, appliances and other equipment, counters, floors, ceilings, walls, window treatment and decor—wiring, electricity and gas supply are key factors. Before you complete your decision-making, it is wise to take time to study these components and understand the part each plays in the kitchen plan.

WIRING AND ELECTRICITY. Wiring, lighting, plumbing and ventilation are the basic elements that supply the working resources necessary for a kitchen to function smoothly. In most of these areas, it is wise to seek professional advice. For wiring, consult a good technician or wiring expert. Arrange for these first, especially if you're remodeling in stages. But, if you've a corner-cutting budget, this is *not* the time to do it. If you are having someone do the entire job, these services will be included in the subcontracting.

A new kitchen should be planned to provide an ample power supply for today and the future and to wisely conserve as much energy as possible.

Geographical locations and community codes determine wiring specifications. Check with local electricians for your particular needs. Local utility companies also may offer wiring advice and will supply wiring plans, either free or for a nominal fee.

Make certain a qualified electrician verifies that:

- Adequate electric service is available for electrical products.
- The addition of the appliance(s) will not overload any individual circuit on which it is used.
- Appliance circuits have adequately grounded, three-hole receptacles.
- Grounded outlets are properly polarized.

Most modern homes are supplied with a three-wire (240-volt) service entrance with a capacity of 100 amperes or more. The wattage available is calculated by multiplying the number of amperes by the number of volts. For efficient use of electricity, a load not greater than 80 percent of capacity is recommended. For a 100-ampere, 240-volt circuit, the maximum recommended capacity is 100x240x.80 which equals 19,200 watts.

The household electrical supply is divided into separate circuits at the distribution center (fuse or circuit-breaker box). Three kinds of circuits are provided: (1) lighting and general purpose—120-volt, 15-ampere; (2) appliance—120-volt, 20-ampere; (3) individual—voltage and amperage as required by the appliance connected to the circuit.

Fuses or circuit-breakers should match the capacity of the wire in the circuit.

Most 120-volt major appliances, such as a refrigerator, have a three-wire cord and a three-pronged plug to ground the appliance and protect against shock hazard; it should be connected to a properly grounded three-hole outlet. A two-hole wall receptacle must be replaced with a properly grounded three-hole receptacle by a qualified electrician.

Check your wiring needs with the chart below for major and small appliances, lighting and ventilation. Be sure to include enough convenience outlets and sufficient current.

CIRCUITRY	USE
1. One 240-volt circuit each	Electric range. Built-in electric oven and cooktop. Electric dryer. Air conditioner.
2. One 120-volt circuit each	Refrigerator-freezer combination. Freezer. Dishwasher and disposer. Washer.
3. Two 120-volt, 20-ampere circuits	Small appliances. Gas range. Automatic ice maker. Compact refrigerator. Trash compactor.
4. One 120-volt, 15-ampere circuit	Lights. Clock. Exhaust fan. Radio. Television. Sewing machine.

5. Plan on one duplex outlet for every 4 feet of counter space or plug-in wiring strips, placed at a convenient height for intended use.

GAS REQUIREMENTS. Input to gas appliances is controlled through a gas appliance pressure regulator and by the use of proper-sized openings. Upon installation or if you change from one type of gas to another (bottled to natural, for instance, or vice versa), consult a qualified technician to be certain that the openings and pressure regulator provide the proper flow of gas.

Gas appliances require air for combustion, and clearance requirements, as shown on the appliance rating plate, should be adhered to.

Check the manufacturer's installation instructions. If the connection must be made to a vent or chimney, the instructions should be followed carefully. The vent should be free from obstructions and inspected annually by the gas company or an authorized service technician.

Improperly adjusted gas appliances can produce carbon monoxide and, therefore, if venting is not correct, carbon monoxide may enter your home.

Wiring for gas appliances, which use an external electrical supply, should be grounded and wired in the same way as for electrical appliances.

8 | Doing It Yourself

Now that you've done your homework and have a pretty good idea of what you want your new kitchen to look like, the time has come to decide how you will achieve it.

You have several options, but, before you exercise any one of them, it would be a good idea in any case if you learn how to draw up your own plans. The degree of refinement will depend upon whether you plan to rely upon yourself entirely or bring in some help. After you have roughed up a floor plan, then you can decide which of three options you would like to follow.

1. Draw up your own plans, subcontract the electrical work and plumbing, buy (or build) your own cabinets and countertops and install them yourself.

2. Draw up your own plans, buy (or build) your own cabinets, then turn the entire job over to a contractor.

3. Have a professional execute the entire job—design your kitchen, order supplies and supervise the installation.

DESIGNING YOUR KITCHEN. This is the time to begin to picture your new kitchen on paper. First, draw a scaled floor plan to give yourself an idea of how it will look. You don't need an architect's degree to do this because we will take you step by step through the various stages of design. There is only one caution to keep in mind. As you measure, be as accurate as you can because even a few inches variation can make a critical difference between choosing one model appliance or another.

Accurate measurement is particularly important if your new kitchen is a do-it-yourself project and you are ordering and selecting all appliances and cabinetry. But do have your cabinet dealer check the plan against the cabinets you are buying. If you are having a professional do the job, then he will be drawing his own plans and can double check your figures. Even if you are having a professional kitchen designer do the work for you, having a scaled floor plan will help you to better interpret just what you have in mind.

Assemble the tools you'll be using: a flexible steel tape measure, pencil, graph paper scaled ¼- to ½-inch per foot (I find this easier than a ⅜-inch scale) and a scaled rule.

Measure the room

• Begin at any corner about 36 inches from the floor and measure along the wall from corner to corner. Mark specific measurements from corner to window, window including trim, etc., and any doors. Measure around the entire room, including all walls, windows, doors, openings and wall jogs. Be sure to include window and door casings as you take the measurements. See illustrations below.

- Include windowsill to floor measurements, door swing and direction.
- Indicate wall thickness; mark irregularities, such as closets, pipelines, chimneys, radiators, registers, wall gaps, etc.
- Indicate location and height of light switches, electrical, plumbing and gas outlets.
- Note ceiling height—floor to ceiling–direction of room and wall placement (north, east, south or west, etc.), appliances you will be keeping, new appliances you plan to add.

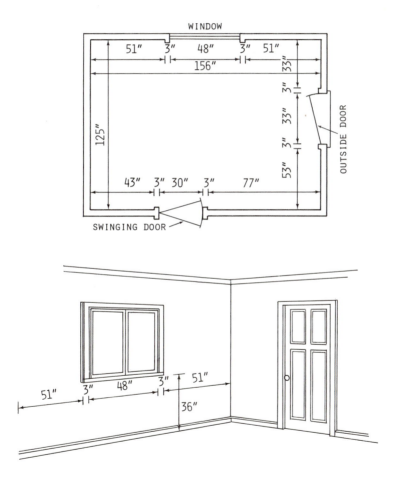

- As you measure, study the wall functions. Do they conceal electrical wiring, gas or water piping, metal duct work, chimneys? If you are designing a kitchen in a new house, look at the blueprint. Structural changes should take load-bearing walls into consideration. Naturally, it would be less costly to avoid making changes in load-bearing walls.

• When you have finished taking all the measurements, check your figures by adding the individual units. They should add up to the overall wall dimension.

On making structural changes

1. Plan structural changes carefully and thoughtfully.

2. What may seem like a major expenditure now could be even more costly if you wait until later, especially since you are making a major investment in the new kitchen and will gain increased efficiency.

3. Always check to see if a wall you are planning to move is a load-bearing one. It may be essential to the overall support or operations of the house.

4. Keep doors in the kitchen to a minimum and position them to direct traffic flow away from major kitchen work area.

5. Window areas, if possible, should equal approximately one fourth of the floor area.

Working measurements

• Allow a minimum of 10 to 14 linear feet of base cabinet storage and 10 linear feet of wall cabinet storage.

• Allow 6 square feet of shelf space for each person. Plan an additional 12 square feet if you entertain a lot.

• Counter space: 18 inches on the latch side of refrigerator. 36 to 42 inches for the mixing center. 36 inches on right side of sink. 30 to 32 inches on left side of sink (with a dishwasher, 24 inches is ample). 24 inches on both sides of range, if possible.

• If a counter turns a corner, allow at least: 9 inches between edge of sink and turn of counter. 14 inches from center of cooktop to turn. 16 inches from latch side of refrigerator to turn. 12 to 14 inches on each side of corner to a fixed appliance. (This will allow installation of corner base cabinet with fixed or revolving shelves.) 27 inches on both walls to turn a corner.

• To work efficiently, consider these clearances: 15 to 18 inches above countertops are FHA requirements for spacing wall cabinets. 6- to 7-inch-deep shelves may be installed just below wall cabinets for small items, spices, etc. 4 inches for separate counter backsplash, or cover entire wall with countertop material. Standard wall cabinets range from 30 to 33 inches high. Standard base cabinets are 34½ inches high and countertops are 1½ inches higher; total counter height is 36 inches. Base cabinets have a 4-inch toe-in space. Plan desks or kitchen buffets require base cabinets measuring 28¼ inches high. Overall cabinet height (base plus wall cabinets) is 84 to 87 inches from floor. For maximum use of top shelf in wall cabinet, hang so top is no more than 72 inches from floor. Utilize tops of cabinets for soffits if more storage space is required. (See page 89.) Utility cabinets are 84 inches tall and 12 or 24 inches deep. Cabinet widths range from 9 to 48 inches in 3-inch increments. Provide a clearance of 4 feet between opposite work areas and 3 feet for passageways.

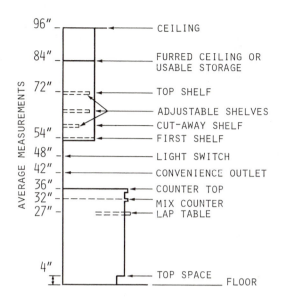

AVERAGE MEASUREMENTS

96" — CEILING

84" — FURRED CEILING OR USABLE STORAGE

72" — TOP SHELF

ADJUSTABLE SHELVES

CUT-AWAY SHELF

54" — FIRST SHELF

48" — LIGHT SWITCH

42" — CONVENIENCE OUTLET

36" — COUNTER TOP

32" — MIX COUNTER

27" — LAP TABLE

4" — TOP SPACE

FLOOR

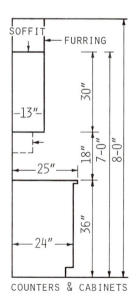

SOFFIT

FURRING

13"

30"

25"

18" 7'-0" 8'-0"

24"

36"

COUNTERS & CABINETS

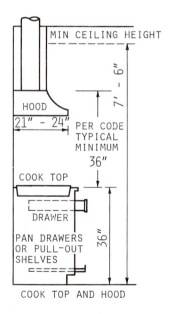

MIN CEILING HEIGHT

7' - 6"

HOOD

21" - 24" PER CODE TYPICAL MINIMUM

36"

COOK TOP

DRAWER

PAN DRAWERS OR PULL-OUT SHELVES

36"

COOK TOP AND HOOD

Working measurements for planning your kitchen.

Drawing the plan to scale

• Using graph paper, and the template opposite, begin drawing your plan. Many cabinet or appliance manufacturers supply templates and drawing instructions for their kitchen customers, if you would prefer to use one of these.

• Note the architectural symbols below. Draw them onto your plan to help your dealer or contractor understand the technical details of your room.

• Determine the shape of your floor plan—U-Shape, L-Shape, Two-Wall or One-Wall. Do you want an island or peninsula?

• Position the sink, range and refrigerator, according to the kitchen work triangle. Don't forget the work centers and how you like to work—from right to left or vice versa? Don't forget the need to direct traffic flow away from the main work area.

• Locate all other appliances such as dishwasher, trash compactor, etc.

• Consider other centers you want to include: a plan desk, laundry area, bar sink, eating area, sitting area.

• Position the cabinets. Floor plans show base cabinets first. Using the template, draw in the wall cabinets over the base cabinets.

• Experiment with your plan. Try different arrangements. Change the positions of appliances and cabinets. The template makes this easy to do. Should a window or door be moved?

• Transfer all measurements accurately from your rough plan. At the side, indicate floor-to-ceiling height and distance from floor to bottom of windowsill. This information will be important to a professional designer and/or contractor.

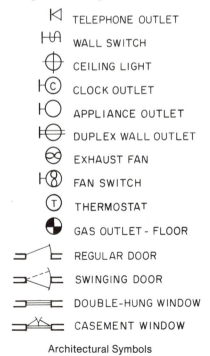

Architectural Symbols

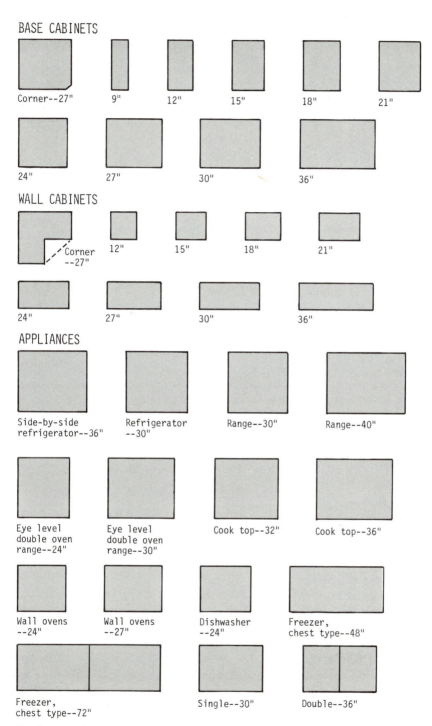

BASE CABINETS

Corner--27" 9" 12" 15" 18" 21"

24" 27" 30" 36"

WALL CABINETS

Corner --27" 12" 15" 18" 21"

24" 27" 30" 36"

APPLIANCES

Side-by-side refrigerator--36" Refrigerator --30" Range--30" Range--40"

Eye level double oven range--24" Eye level double oven range--30" Cook top--32" Cook top--36"

Wall ovens --24" Wall ovens --27" Dishwasher --24" Freezer, chest type--48"

Freezer, chest type--72" Single--30" Double--36"

Use these scaled templates with a sheet of ¼-inch graph paper to plan your kitchen. Additional templates on next page. *Courtesy Electric Energy Assoc.*

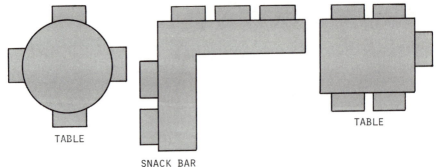

TABLE

SNACK BAR

TABLE

Check your kitchen plan

Answer *yes* or *no* to each of these questions.

( ) Have you designed your plan to minimize traffic flow in work areas?

( ) If you have installed appliances away from the general work area, have you provided counter space nearby?

( ) Are there pull-out shelves, drawers or revolving shelves for ease in storing and retrieving items from base cabinets?

( ) Does work flow move in one direction—right for right-handers, left for left-handers?

( ) Is surface between work counters continuous?

( ) Have you avoided separating counters with doors?

( ) Are work areas multipurpose?

( ) Is there at least 3 feet of space for people to walk around each other comfortably?

( ) If more than one person works in the kitchen at one time, is there adequate space to work at adjacent counters which form a right angle?

( ) Do open appliance doors avoid obstacles?

( ) Have you provided plumbing for refrigerators with ice makers and water chillers?

( ) Is lighting adequate?

( ) Are there enough convenience outlets placed adequately apart?

( ) Have you adequate space for trash, hanging towels, kitchen stool, cart and other conveniences?

( ) Have you considered everything that you might plan to do in the kitchen and provided facilities for it?

If you have answered YES to every question, you are pretty close to the kitchen you'll be comfortable in. If you have any NO answers, go back and check your plan!

INSTALLING CABINETS. It's not difficult if you are so inclined. Many people have done it successfully and have achieved professional results. Several cabinet manufacturers provide illustrated booklets on do-it-yourself cabinet installation. If you decide to buy their cabinetry, they will give you whatever additional advice you need.

Information and illustrations courtesy Yorktowne Kitchens.

Be sure you know exactly what wall and base cabinets look like. You can identify them by the sketches below.

These are standard cabinets; dimensions never change. Wall cabinets are all 12 inches deep and all base cabinets are 34½ inches high and 24 inches deep. Also shown are parts often referred to in installation—*horizontal strips* or *rails* and *vertical strips* or *stiles*.

The big question is what to do yourself and what to leave for the professional. Installing a kitchen is not a job to be undertaken by amateurs, without knowing some of the pitfalls involved.

WALL CABINETS   BASE CABINETS

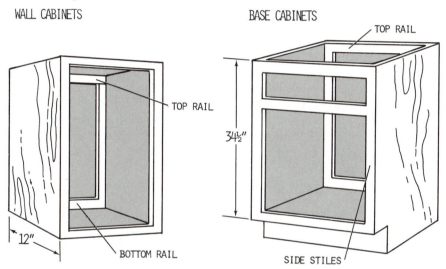

This is not to say that you cannot get help with a plan and then do some or even most of the work yourself. Many leading kitchen dealers encourage do-it-yourself installation. Some even conduct do-it-yourself courses. They also offer these tips:

1. Know what you're getting into. Cabinet installation is one thing, but electrical work and plumbing is another. It is wise to leave these to the professionals. And remember that, unless some appliances are installed by an authorized servicer, warranties could be voided.
2. Make certain you have the time and the talent for do-it-yourself installation.
3. Use your time wisely. Demolition of your existing kitchen is an either/or chore. Ripping out old cabinets and countertops can be immensely satisfying to some, but to you it may be less so than installing new cabinets. Doing what you enjoy is faster work than what you find boring.
5. Know what you are buying. Check specification sheets and become familiar with measurements.
6. Familiarize yourself with local building codes and permit requirements.

Whatever your decision, read all the instructions carefully before you begin to do any work. Get all the information together and run through the entire installation on paper. This will help you to work out any bugs before you begin, or to figure out answers to questions you may have. Above all, be patient!

On paper, follow the cabinet manufacturer's special instructions for the cabinetry you would like to have. They should be in a position to give you the necessary guidelines for planning a layout and ordering the cabinets. Or, follow the instructions for designing your own kitchen. Once you have drawn an accurate plan according to the specific measurements of your room, you will begin to see what your requirements are.

When you have decided upon your final plan, have selected the cabinets and the cabinet dealer, take your plan in for consultation. Discuss the plan with your dealer's kitchen expert. Ask any questions that you may have on your mind. Ask for any literature about the line you have selected. Read it carefully and become familiar with the cabinets you would like to order.

After you have listed all the cabinets you need, then place your order and devise a work plan, based upon the proposed delivery schedule.

Next, you should check out all your plumbing, electrical, metal and ducting requirements. It's a good idea to bring in professional contractors for these jobs as they have the technical expertise. This is a crucial part of your remodeling and it should be done correctly and early. You may have to change a plumbing line or update your wiring to accommodate additional appliances or improve your work area. This is the time to remove old plumbing and install the new, and to make any strategic, structural changes you may need assistance with.

The tools

Make certain you have armed yourself with the proper tools. You will need:

A tape measure or folding rule.	Framing square.
Carpenter's level.	Stepladder.
Claw hammer.	Chalkline.
¼-inch electric drill with bits and countersink.	Carpenter's plane (optional).
	Saw (optional).
Screwdrivers (Phillips and regular).	Stud finder (optional).
Awl (or scribing tool).	Crowbar (optional).
Two C-clamps (4-inch clamping space).	

Materials

1¾-inch and 2½-inch #8 flathead wood screws for wood cabinets.
Metal screws, if installing metal cabinets.
Cedar wood builder's shims (from lumber dealer).
Straightedge (6 feet, two-by-four, no warps).
Several 8-foot x 1½-inch x ¾-inch furring strips (for building supports, etc.).
Glue (optional).
Touch-up kit (from cabinet dealer; optional).
Patching plaster (and plaster stick; optional).
Fine and medium sandpaper (optional).
Metal L-braces (optional).

Preparing for installation. Now the preparation stage begins. If you are installing cabinets in a new home, then the next few steps will not apply to you. If you are remodeling the kitchen in your present home, remove all the old cabinets. Remove the major appliances that will be involved in the remodeling. Reconnect the refrigerator in an adjacent or nearby room for continued use. (This is the perfect time to have any plumbing, wiring or metal duct work done, after the contractors have advised you of your needs and supplied the estimates.) Remove all the old countertops. Countertops are usually fastened with screws driven up through the frame of the base cabinet into the old top. If it has been nailed, pry it up with a crowbar.

If you plan to use your present sink, it will have to be disconnected before the countertop is removed. Remove any existing baseboards where you plan to install cabinets in a new area. Remove the flooring at this time, if you plan to install a new one.

Before you install new flooring, cover old boards with plywood or a surface recommended by the flooring dealer. Be certain the floor is level by shimming low spots with scrap lumber. After you have done all this, you are ready to begin cabinet installation.

It is essential that cabinets are mounted both level and square. (*Note:* Cabinets may be pulled out of square when installed to walls with irregular or uneven surfaces. When this happens, cabinet doors appear to be warped or hung out of line. The fault probably lies in the forced twisting of the cabinet frame and not in the cabinet itself.)

Many floors and walls, both old and new, are not level. It is important that you follow the next steps very carefully to insure a professional-looking installation.

The tops of wall cabinets are generally installed 84 inches above floor level. Locate this height from the highest point of the floor. Find the high point by using a carpenter's level or a straightedge. Check the width of the room first for the high point. Next check the level of the floor at this point, 21 inches from the wall. If the floor, 21 inches away from the wall, is higher, mark this height on the wall.

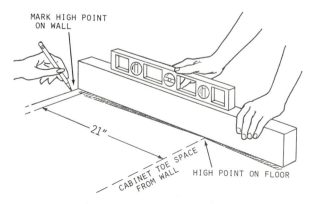

MARK HIGH POINT ON WALL

21"

CABINET TOE SPACE FROM WALL   HIGH POINT ON FLOOR

Then, proceed up the wall and mark off the 84-inch height and, using the level and straightedge, continue this line around the room. This line will show the location of the tops of the wall cabinets at 84 inches above floor level. Mark another horizontal line on the wall at 34½ inches above the high point to locate the tops of the base cabinets.

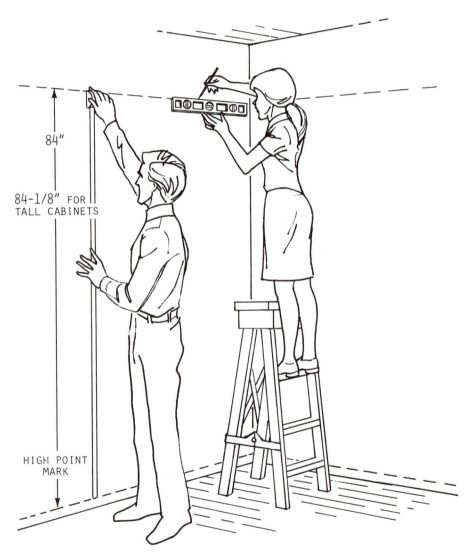

You are ready now to mark the walls for each cabinet. Begin at any corner, and fix the position of each cabinet by marking its exact location. This is simply double-checking to make certain your layout is accurate.

Soffits. If you are planning to install a soffit, see drawing below and on p. 90 for styles. Allow an 84⅛-inch clearance if your plan calls for any 84-inch-high, floor-to-soffit cabinets, commonly called utility cabinets. The ⅛-inch provides clearance to fit the tall cabinet under the soffit. This clearance space will be covered with the trim molding, used to trim off the tops of wall cabinets at the soffit. When constructing soffits, keep in mind that wall cabinets are 12 inches deep. A 1-inch soffit overhang should allow ample space for trim molding.

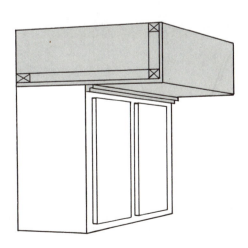

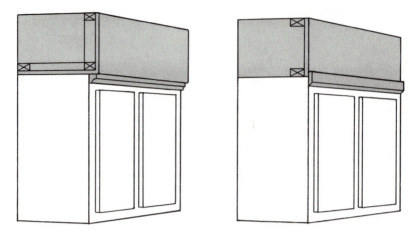

Locating the wall studs. Because it is extremely important to support wall cabinets to a solid mounting, take time now to find the wall studs. Look for them with a stud finder—a magnetic device which locates nails. If you don't have a stud finder, tap the wall to find a solid sound. This should indicate a stud installation. Test it by driving a thin nail into the stud. They are usually installed 16 inches apart. When you have located the center of each stud, mark a vertical line to indicate the position for securing the cabinets.

Remember: Always secure cabinets into a solid mounting—never into plasterboard with molly screws.

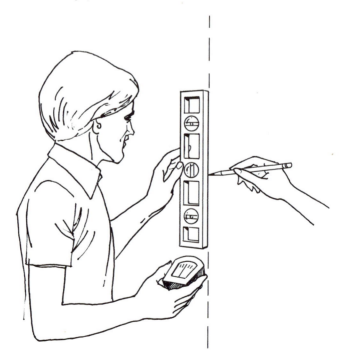

Installing the wall cabinets. Begin with the corner wall cabinets. Support the cabinet with the top aligned to the 84-inch-high mark. Drill through the inside horizontal strips into the wall studs and fasten the cabinet top and bottom with 2½-inch screws. (Use wood screws for wood cabinets, metal screws for metal cabinets.)

Tip: To help you in the installation of wall cabinets, construct a simple T-brace. Use it to support the cabinets at the desired height until they are fastened to the wall studs.

Make certain the cabinet is plumb on both sides and front. Use your carpenter's level to determine if cabinets are level vertically and horizontally.

If the walls are uneven, *never* drive the screws tight until you are sure the cabinet is level and square. If necessary, shim out the cabinets with builder's shims or thin strips of wood so they will remain square when screws are driven tight. You will find some examples of how shims should be used on page 93.

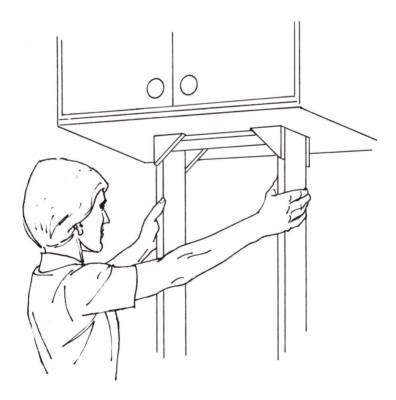

Wall fillers are used to "fill-in" or compensate for odd dimensions and to allow for clearance where cabinets meet at corners. They may be sawed or planed to the exact measurement needed for a precise fit. Attach fillers to adjoining cabinets by drilling very carefully through side stiles or by using cleats.

Continue working away from corner units, checking all along that each cabinet is square and level. Add shims whenever they are needed. Attach wall cabinets to each other by drilling and screwing through the inside vertical strips or stiles of the cabinet front frame. Use C-clamps freely to hold the vertical strips securely together while the holes are being drilled and screws driven. To protect finished cabinet surfaces from C-clamp marks, use scrap-wood strips under the clamp.

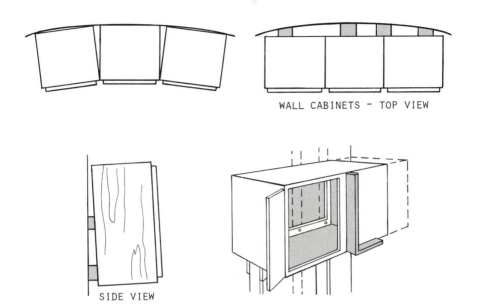

WALL CABINETS – TOP VIEW

SIDE VIEW

Cabinets installed on a concave wall (top) must be shimmed to compensate for the recess. Cabinets on a sloping wall (above left) must be shimmed so they are vertical. Wall fillers are used where cabinets meet at a corner (above right).

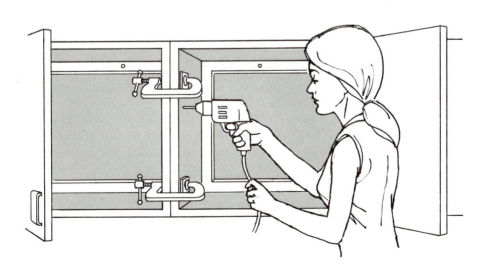

Installing base cabinets. Again, as for wall cabinet installation, check the evenness of the walls. Do not secure the screws completely, until you have determined if the cabinet is level and square. To keep it square, use builder's shims as you did for the wall cabinets.

Here are examples of shims used in base cabinet installations.

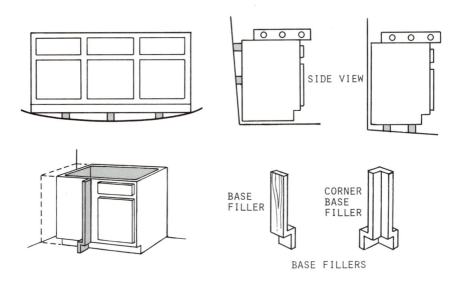

SIDE VIEW

BASE
FILLER

CORNER
BASE
FILLER

BASE FILLERS

Base cabinets must be shimmed to compensate for irregular floors and walls (top). When cabinets meet at a corner, use filler as shown above left.

Use fillers to compensate for odd dimensions and provide for clearance where cabinets meet at corners. Saw or plane them to the exact fit and attach them to the adjoining cabinet by drilling through the side stiles or by using cleats.

Some revolving, corner base cabinets are barrel-shaped and will not fit the right angle of the corner. A barrel-shaped cabinet requires 36 inches of space on each wall. Locate it by lining it up with the adjoining cabinet which is 36 inches from the corner. These cabinets must be level for proper operation. An off-level installation will cause revolving doors to scrape on sides or bottom.

To install regular base cabinets, align and secure their back horizontal strips or top rails at the 34½-inch-high level you marked on the wall. Again, just as you did with the wall cabinets, align and level them horizontally and vertically, using any shims necessary behind and under the cabinets to fill out the empty spaces. Attach the base cabinets to each other through the side strips or stiles of the front frames as in the wall cabinets.

INSTALLING COUNTERTOPS. Countertops are 1½ inches thick to bring them to the standard 36-inch appliance height. You can order countertop blanks in standard 6-, 8- and 12-foot lengths or have them custom-made through your cabinet dealer.

To install a countertop, place it on the cabinets and check the alignment with cabinets and walls. It should have a 1-inch overhang in the front and at the ends of the cabinets, except where adjacent to appliances. Attach the countertop to the cabinets with 1¾-inch-long screws, which extend through the cabinet corner blocks into the bottom frame of the countertop. Any space for drop-in units, such as a range and sink, is cut in after the countertop has been fastened to the cabinets.

Exercise caution in using the drill. Make certain that you do not drill through the countertop.

You may wish to install a metal cove molding behind the backsplash of the top to compensate for any imperfections in the fit between the wall and countertop.

ALIGNMENT OF DOORS AND DRAWERS. When you have completed the installation of all wall and base cabinets, it may be that some of the door and drawer fronts are not parallel with each other. If this is true, you need to align them.

To align doors, remove the hinge screws from the door or cabinet frame, depending on which way you want to move the door. Visually determine how much you wish to tilt the door at top or bottom. Fill the old screw holes with a wood matchstick or a ⅛-inch dowel and drill a hole at the new, determined location. Replace old screw in the new hole.

To align drawers, determine the amount of correction necessary at top or bottom. If drawers have removable drawer fronts, remove the drawer front from the drawer box. Fill holes with a wood dowel and drill a new hole; replace screws.

FINISHING. When you have completed the final work, remove any fingerprints and marks which have resulted from handling and installation.

Avoid the use of abrasive cleaners or strong detergents. Some household waxes contain agents designed to cut dirt, and these may damage fine furniture finishes. Use a wax recommended by the cabinet manufacturer. Apply it with a soft cloth and rub hard enough to apply a smooth finish. Put a little extra wax on the bottom edge of base cabinets and base cabinet doors, where invisible moisture may collect. Always wipe cabinets dry immediately, if they become wet.

9 | Hiring a Professional

No DOUBT YOU have your finished floor plan in front of you and have made the endless lists we have recommended. You have done your comparison shopping and have a pretty good idea of how you would like to proceed. If you have decided to do the job yourself, if you have ordered (or made) your cabinetry and have checked the plan and delivery schedule with your cabinet dealer, your instructions for installation have been covered. But if you have decided to bring in a professional to do the entire job, you've still some planning ahead of you.

There are a variety of technical people who are qualified to help you with your kitchen. They offer a variety of services, from executing the entire job to simply doing one phase of the job, leaving you to do the rest or have it subcontracted. Whoever you select, make certain that they are specialists in designing and installing kitchens. It will save money in the long run, even though you may have to pay a little extra at the outset for professional expertise. They are experienced in the technicalities of drawing and executing a floor plan, ordering materials and working with subcontractors. A kitchen specialist can help you maximize space and cost efficiency. (See listing of specialists at the end of this chapter.)

Whatever you do, follow these three steps:
1. Measure your kitchen and draw it to scale. See pages 78–82.
2. Draw up a rough plan and indicate *all* the measurements—thickness of walls, door and window widths, door swing, placement of plumbing and electrical outlets, etc.
3. Shop the market and know who and where the professionals are and what materials and equipment you might like to use.

As you shop around, interview candidates and compare showrooms. In your search for a professional, get answers to these questions:
1. Is there a qualified kitchen designer to plan the kitchen?
2. Can they take on the entire remodeling from beginning to end?
3. Who is responsible for guaranteeing the work? What kind of guarantee do they offer?
4. Are they franchised or authorized dealers of specific products and services?

Show prospective candidates your rough floor plans. Check client references and study portfolios showing completed installations. Ask for estimates and get a firm and fixed fee for the entire job. Ask about contracts, make sure everything is in it and check all facts carefully.

THE PROFESSIONAL IN YOUR KITCHEN. When you have decided on your kitchen dealer and know what kind of cabinetry you want, ask the dealer or salesperson to come to your home. This is interview time. The dealer or salesperson will coordinate the information you have listed and sorted out in all the early-stage check lists. He will make copious notes, take measurements and your rough plan ideas back to the designer who will draw up a finished plan and estimate for your approval.

In the showroom. When this presentation is complete, you will take time to go into the showroom for a final meeting. During the presentation you will look at:

- Final floor plans.
- Perspective drawings.
- Samples.
- Hardware.

- Swatches of materials.
- Color selections.
- Fabric.

Take time now to discuss all the details. Ask questions. Make changes. Do all this *before*, not *after*, you sign a contract. Develop a satisfactory and mutually agreeable work schedule from start to finish. Discuss finances and how you plan to make the payments. When you have all this information clearly in mind, you are ready for the contract. Read it carefully and make certain you understand all its ramifications. Then, sign on the dotted line!

The dealer. Now, it's your dealer's turn to take over—order all materials, subcontract the various jobs with tradesmen and organize the schedule for installation. The deadlines for completion depend upon the kind of plan, where you are on the dealer's priority list, and whether or not you've ordered stock or custom-designed cabinetry. Stock cabinetry may be readily available from a week to ten days; custom-designed cabinets may require six to eight weeks delivery.

The part you play. You will be notified when the work is about to begin. When you receive this notice, clear out the kitchen of everything that will be an obstacle to the workmen. Pick a spot nearby where you can put everything and where you can find it readily if you need it. Cover up furniture in adjoining rooms. Apply masking tape around inside doors to confine the dust to the work area.

If your entire kitchen is to be dismantled, make arrangements to connect your refrigerator in another room and organize an area for short-order cooking. Leave out a coffee maker, griddle, electric skillet and a toaster-oven. They'll come in handy for short-order cooking all during the installation period.

It's a good idea to ask for a copy of the work schedule so you will know what is happening each day. Electricity, gas and water may be turned off at different periods.

You can most likely expect the kitchen dealer or dealer salesman to be there the first day of the installation and to supervise the work from time to time. Certainly, the dealer representative will be there on the last day of installation to check out every detail with you. Make certain you are completely satisfied with every detail before you make the last payment.

SPECIALIST	QUALIFICATION AND SERVICES OFFERED
KITCHEN DEALERS	Specialists in kitchen remodeling and installation. Have a showroom displaying model kitchens, materials, appliances, equipment and supplies. Excellent qualifications to take on entire job from planning to installation. Some may offer decorating services. Usually will remodel bathrooms, laundries and other areas. Ask to see client references and portfolio.
	Leading dealers are members of AIKD—the American Institute of Kitchen Dealers. Member requirements include proof of performance, financial responsibility, written declaration of professional status, documented business history, display of AIKD Standards of Conduct, and provision of a one-year warranty upon completion of client's work.
	Best specialists—either dealer and/or one or more employees qualify as a CKD (Certified Kitchen Designer). To be a CKD, one must qualify on basis of oral and written examination, and submit affidavits from clients and other professionals to the industry's accrediting body, the Council of Certified Kitchen Designers.
	Some dealers charge a fee for the original estimate, including a home visit, personal interview, preliminary measurements, plan and specifications. Fee is credited to total cost if contracted to do job.
CABINET MANUFACTURERS	Many have local retail outlets offering kitchen planning services.
	Many leading kitchen dealers described above are franchised to carry specific cabinet manufacturer's lines and have the same qualifications described above.
DEPARTMENT STORES	Some of the larger ones have kitchen planning departments. Usually managed by kitchen planning or remodeling specialists.
	May have displays and model kitchens; also kitchen planning specialists. Specialists may have same qualifications as kitchen dealers, described above.
	Ask to see a client reference and a portfolio of completed jobs.
BUILDING SUPPLY OR LUMBER DEALERS	Generally sell supplies and equipment for kitchen and home improvement remodelings. May or may not have a design and installation service.
	Many can help you arrange for subcontractors if you are doing most of the work yourself. If you subcontract through building supply or lumber dealers, get commitment in writing as to whose responsibility it is for specific jobs—what and how they will do it, what it will cost and who will guarantee what.
HOME IMPROVEMENT CENTERS REMODELING CONTRACTORS	Interior and exterior remodelings, including kitchens and baths.
	If they are doing an entire remodeling, it may be less expensive to have them do the kitchen also. Leading remodeling contractors are members of the National Remodeler's Association or the National Home Improvement Council.

SPECIALIST	QUALIFICATION AND SERVICES OFFERED
CABINETMAKERS	Make cabinets in their workshops or on the site; will install. Some may do entire remodeling and be responsible for subcontracting. May be members of National Remodeler's Association or the National Home Improvement Council.
PLUMBING AND ELECTRICAL CONTRACTORS	May qualify as kitchen specialists, if they have showrooms and specialists to design kitchens and supervise remodelings.
HEATING, SHEET METAL, FLOORING, TILE AND MASONRY CONTRACTORS	Strictly subcontractors for specialty fields.
APPLIANCE DEALERS	Sell appliances only. Some may have kitchen planning specialists. Provide optional installation service.
ARCHITECTS	Usually plan kitchens in connection with total house. Some may take on individual kitchen remodelings; others prefer not to. Well qualified to plan kitchens and do remodelings.
INTERIOR DESIGNERS	Will do kitchens along with total refurbishing. May take on individual kitchen remodeling. Familiar with materials, but generally not technically oriented. Will subcontract most of the work.
UTILITY COMPANIES	May offer kitchen planning, lighting and wiring services.

10 | Design an Energy-Efficient Kitchen

As you complete final plans for your new kitchen, it is time to focus on the impact the *energy crisis* has had upon the selection and operation of your appliances.

Shopping for an appliance today is not the comparatively easy job it once was several years ago when price and personal preference of special features were primary considerations. Today, top priorities include fuel source, energy consumption and operating costs. When shopping for an appliance today, it is important to keep in mind that while the price tag plays an important part in your decision, it tells only one-third of the story. What it doesn't tell is what it will cost to operate the appliance month after month or what the maintenance costs will be. As energy costs continue to increase, we need more information on operating costs, and more importantly on the appliance's energy efficiency.

THE ENERGY IMPACT. We are all aware that there does exist an energy crisis. We are told at every turn that ours is a "high energy" economy, with increasing energy consumption and rising energy prices. Certainly that's a major issue that concerns us all.

According to the experts, world fossil-fuel reserves appear adequate for at least the next half century. Therefore our short-term concern is not the availability of fossil fuels but temporary shortages and increased costs. Utilities are forced to charge higher rates for energy owing to higher environmental protection standards and skyrocketing construction costs. Federal energy programming is encouraging, indeed mandating, appliance manufacturers to produce more efficient home appliances and at the same time encouraging consumers to purchase these more efficient appliances. What effect, then, will appliance efficiency have upon energy consumption? How can our individual decisions on appliance selection and more efficient use of these appliances affect total energy consumption?

According to a research study made in 1968, industry consumed 41.2% of our energy supply and transportation 25.2%; commercial consumption amounted to 14.4% and residential uses totaled 19.2%. Taking a closer look at residential uses in this study, and focusing specifically upon home and kitchen functions, we find that lighting and all other functions consumed 2.2%, air conditioning 1%, refrigeration 1%, cooking 1%, water heating 3% and space heating 11%.

Obviously, space heating and water heating account for 14%—the bulk of residential use. The major kitchen functions of refrigeration and cooking each consume 1% of total U.S. energy supply. Lighting, air conditioning and all other residential functions consume the remaining 3.2%.

In another, more current study published by the Department of Energy, the same pattern of energy consumption is analyzed differently. Based on an average household's energy consumption, we note that space heating consumes 63.5%, water heating 18.4%, cooking 5.9%, refrigeration 3.2%, space cooling 2.7%, lighting 2.2%, clothes drying 1.5%, all others 2.6%. Space heating and water heating head the list of high energy users once again. Cooking, refrigeration, space cooling and clothes drying, those functions most closely allied with kitchens and similar areas, total less than one-seventh of the energy used in an average household.

While more efficient appliances will account for a small fraction of the solution to the nation's energy problem, nevertheless they will contribute collectively to the conservation of the total energy picture.

DETERMINING APPLIANCE EFFICIENCY. You may be wondering if different appliances can make that much difference in energy consumption. They can. Your choice of one refrigerator over another, for example, may result in a 50% higher cost of operation. But how can you make a wise choice?

In 1980 labels containing energy information began to appear on major home appliances. The labeling program is under the direction of the Federal Trade Commission. Look for the labels on refrigerators, refrigerator-freezers, freezers, dishwashers, water heaters, room air conditioners, clothes washers and furnaces. Originally consideration was given to labeling clothes dryers, ranges and ovens, and television sets, but it was determined that the labeling of these products would be of little value to the shopper.

Each energy label includes:

1. Estimated annual energy cost.
2. Range of energy costs or efficiencies for similar models.
3. Energy efficiency as determined in tests developed by the Department of Energy.
4. Description of the particular appliance model.
5. Tables affording the consumer opportunity to estimate individual yearly costs depending upon frequency of use and local utility rate.

The purpose of the energy label is to give you, the shopper, the opportunity to consider energy cost in an ultimate purchasing decision. Using the label properly, you can compare energy costs along with price, appearance, convenience features and other options. The annual cost of operation is based upon the national average cost of energy and, when applicable, normal consumer usage patterns.

For instance, the cost of the energy consumed washing a load of dishes in an automatic dishwasher can be easily measured. However, it was felt that this information alone was not very meaningful. Therefore, they multiplied the energy consumed per load by the "normal" annual number of loads. If your habits are not "normal," the label also includes a usage chart allowing you to compute the

Department of Energy/Electronics Industries Assn., 1978 *End of Use Energy Consumption Data Base.*

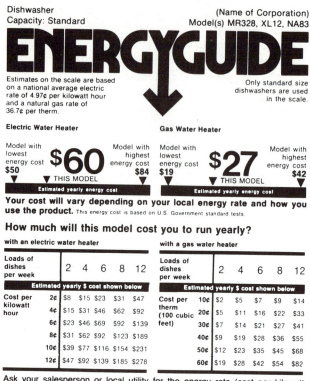

Dishwasher
Capacity: Standard

(Name of Corporation)
Model(s) MR328, XL12, NA83

ENERGYGUIDE

Estimates on the scale are based
on a national average electric
rate of 4.97¢ per kilowatt hour
and a natural gas rate of
36.7¢ per therm.

Only standard size
dishwashers are used
in the scale.

Electric Water Heater

Gas Water Heater

Model with lowest energy cost
$50

$60 THIS MODEL

Model with highest energy cost
$84

Model with lowest energy cost
$19

$27 THIS MODEL

Model with highest energy cost
$42

Estimated yearly energy cost

Estimated yearly energy cost

Your cost will vary depending on your local energy rate and how you use the product. This energy cost is based on U.S. Government standard tests.

How much will this model cost you to run yearly?

with an electric water heater

Loads of dishes per week	2	4	6	8	12
Estimated yearly $ cost shown below					
Cost per kilowatt hour 2¢	$8	$15	$23	$31	$47
4¢	$15	$31	$46	$62	$92
6¢	$23	$46	$69	$92	$139
8¢	$31	$62	$92	$123	$189
10¢	$39	$77	$116	$154	$231
12¢	$47	$92	$139	$185	$278

with a gas water heater

Loads of dishes per week	2	4	6	8	12
Estimated yearly $ cost shown below					
Cost per therm (100 cubic feet) 10¢	$2	$5	$7	$9	$14
20¢	$5	$11	$16	$22	$33
30¢	$7	$14	$21	$27	$41
40¢	$9	$19	$28	$36	$55
50¢	$12	$23	$35	$45	$68
60¢	$19	$28	$42	$54	$82

Ask your salesperson or local utility for the energy rate (cost per kilowatt hour or therm) in your area, and for estimated costs if you have a propane or oil water heater.

Important Removal of this label before consumer purchase is a violation of federal law (42 U.S.C. 6302)

(Part No. 73906)

cost of operation based upon *actual* usage. Also, if your energy cost differs from the national average, the chart allows you to determine the cost of operation based upon your actual energy cost. The label also tells how the energy costs compare with other models with similar features.

For appliances that can use different sources of energy, such as a dishwasher or washing machine, the label will indicate two annual operating-cost figures, ranges of comparability and usage charts. For example, this duplication will allow you to determine cost estimates for the appliance based on whether the hot water supplied to the appliance is heated by a gas or electric water heater.

Taking another example of a refrigerator-freezer label, you will note that Brand X Models AH503, AH504 and AH507 refrigerator/freezers with a capacity of 23 cubic feet have a yearly energy cost of $91. According to the label, this energy cost estimate is based upon a national average electric rate of 4.97¢ per kilowatt hour. Consumers whose electric rates differ from this national average

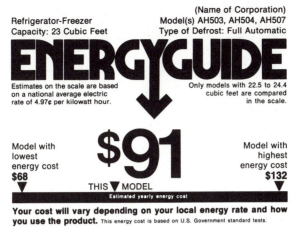

Refrigerator-Freezer
Capacity: 23 Cubic Feet

(Name of Corporation)
Model(s) AH503, AH504, AH507
Type of Defrost: Full Automatic

ENERGYGUIDE

Estimates on the scale are based on a national average electric rate of 4.97¢ per kilowatt hour.

Only models with 22.5 to 24.4 cubic feet are compared in the scale.

Model with lowest energy cost
$68

$91

THIS ▼ MODEL

Estimated yearly energy cost

Model with highest energy cost
$132

Your cost will vary depending on your local energy rate and how you use the product. This energy cost is based on U.S. Government standard tests.

How much will this model cost you to run yearly?

Yearly cost	
Estimated yearly $ cost shown below	
Cost per kilowatt hour	2¢	$44
	4¢	$88
	6¢	$132
	8¢	$176
	10¢	$220
	12¢	$264

Ask your salesperson or local utility for the energy rate (cost per kilowatt hour) in your area.

Important Removal of this label before consumer purchase is a violation of federal law (42 U.S.C. 6302)

(Part No. 371026)

can determine their own average yearly electric cost by locating their cost per kilowatt hour on the chart. The label also tells how the energy costs of this refrigerator compare with other models with similar capacities (22.5 to 24.4 cubic feet). The model with the lowest energy cost is listed on the scale to be $68 and the model with the highest energy cost is listed as $132 per year. This information tells you that the $91 per year cost of operation for this particular model is slightly below average compared to similar models.

An energy-efficient kitchen centers primarily around the three work centers. Each work center is designed around a major appliance, and, with the exception of the range, energy labels are available to make a wise purchasing decision in the interest of increased energy efficiency.

Looking at the key work centers and considering each appliance individually, let's examine some of the features which will help you save energy.

COOKING CENTER: THE RANGE. Your choice of a gas or electric range depends upon personal preference and on fuel availability. Once a purchasing decision is made, brands and models within the same fuel category will vary little in energy consumption.

If a gas range is your preference, select one with an electric ignition, thus eliminating oven and surface-burner pilot lights, which consume additional energy. Most models have an electric ignition.

Careful choice of an oven can also help to curtail energy consumption. Three types of ovens are energy-savers:

Self-cleaning oven. Uses less energy than a standard design, as it is equipped with extra insulation owing to the high temperatures required by the cleaning cycles.

Convection oven. A blower forces heat into the oven and recirculates the air through the system. Only about 10% of the heat is exhausted through the oven vent. In some models, no preheating is necessary. Cooking temperatures can be lowered by about 25% and cooking times can be shorter. Gas-range models can provide energy savings of up to 40%.

Microwave oven. Depending upon the type and amount of food cooked, and frequency of use, this oven can help save energy. Association of Home Appliance Manufacturers' tests found that homes with a standard range and a microwave oven used about 14% less energy than those with only a standard range and oven.

CLEAN-UP CENTER: DISHWASHER. The following features will help you save energy:

Short cycle selections. Shorter cycles use less hot water and are suitable for lightly soiled dishes. You can save up to 25% of water-heating energy costs with short cycles.

Less hot-water usage. Models vary as to the number of gallons of hot water used in a cycle. Check the company's specification sheets, buying guides and other literature for this information.

Built-in water heater. This offers increased efficiency and more heat retention, thus allowing you to lower your home hot-water heater to 120°F, if desired. To insure proper cleaning, sanitizing and drying, recommended temperature for dishwashers is 140°F. By turning down the temperature of the water heater just 20° you can save approximately 10% or more of the energy needed to heat the water for the entire house. This is why it is important to have some facility built into your dishwasher that will increase the water temperature to the recommended 140° at the proper time.

An air-dry selector. This automatically shuts off the heat during the dry cycle. This can save 10% of the electricity. You'll find it on most new models.

Look for the yellow energy label on each dishwasher. It will tell you the estimated yearly operating cost based on how that model performed under laboratory tests and an average national utility rate. It will also give information to help you figure out more closely what it will cost you to operate this particular model, based on the number of dishloads you wash a year and your local utility rate. Try to choose a dishwasher with a low operating cost. The price tag may be somewhat higher but lower utility bills will eventually repay you for the extra money spent.

FOOD PREPARATION CENTER: REFRIGERATOR/FREEZER. Energy consumption of these appliances depends mainly on over-all size, freezer size and temperature, and the type of defrost system. Generally, larger refrigerator/ freezers, especially those with larger freezer compartments, colder freezer temperatures and automatic defrost systems, will use more energy. According to the Association of Home Appliance Manufacturers, these three factors are directly related to the door style.

As far as defrost systems are concerned, there are three types:

1. Manual defrost. The user turns the refrigerator control to *off* or *defrost* to loosen the ice from the surfaces. Defrosted water and ice from both refrigerator and freezer sections are removed manually.

2. Partial automatic or cycle defrost. The cooling surface in the fresh food compartment (refrigerator section) defrosts automatically, but the freezer section must be defrosted manually.

3. Automatic defrost. All frost is removed automatically in both the refrigerator and freezer sections. While automatic defrost capability uses more energy, there are compensations. There will be no frost build-up on freezer surfaces, which, when more than ¼-inch thick, causes a refrigerator to work harder.

If you have a large family and buy food in large quantities; if you live far from a supermarket; if you have a garden and like to freeze foods in quantity; if you prepare foods in advance and do a great deal of entertaining—you should consider buying a large-capacity refrigerator/freezer.

If you live alone and prepare few or small meals, or if you are a couple with no children, choose a smaller model.

Single door refrigerator
Overall size: 1.7 to 14 cubic feet.
Freezer size and temperature: .36 to 2.09 cubic feet; 15°, for ice cubes and short-term food storage.
Defrost system: Most have manual defrost. A few larger ones have partial or automatic defrost.

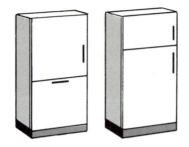

Two-door combination refrigerator-freezer
Overall size: 7.7 to 22.9 cubic feet.
Freezer size and temperature: 1.49 to 7.65 cubic feet; "zero zone" for long-term food storage.
Defrost system: With exception of a few smaller models, all have either partial automatic or automatic defrost systems.

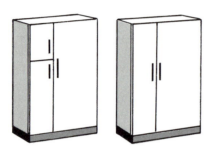

Side-by-side or three-door combination refrigerator-freezer
Overall size: 18.3 to 27.8 cubic feet.
Freezer size and temperature: 6.31 to 10.26 cubic feet; "zero zone" for long-term food storage.
Defrost system: All side-by-side and three-door models have automatic defrost systems.

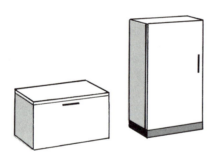

Freezers
Overall size: Chest freezers, 5.1 to 28 cubic feet; upright models, 5.2 to 31.1 cubic feet.
Freezer temperature: All freezers have "zero zone" for long-term food storage.
Defrost system: All chest freezers have manual defrost; a few upright models have automatic defrost systems.

PART II | BUILDING YOUR OWN CABINETS

Introduction

IN THE FIRST part of this book we outlined the process of planning a kitchen remodeling job and suggested several options for getting the work done. If you're on a limited budget, we advised either buying cabinets and installing them yourself, or building your own cabinets. We've already shown you how to install cabinets; this part of the book shows you how to build them. We also explain how to remodel the plumbing and electrical wiring so that your new kitchen can function properly.

There's a do-it-yourself alternative to building your own cabinets, and that's resurfacing the ones you have. The process is explained in detail in the first chapter of this section.

You may wonder whether building your own cabinets is really a saving, considering the time and effort, and the cost of materials. That's easy enough to find out; just add up the prices for cabinets (you can get them from a mail-order house or from a local dealer), then estimate the cost of materials for building your own. You may find there's a considerable spread in cost. But there are other factors to be considered. Very important is the pride of achievement you will enjoy when the job is done. If you wish, you can do the renovation piecemeal, whenever you have the time, and meet the cost as you go without straining your means or borrowing.

You also have the satisfaction of knowing the cabinets are well built. Although there are some well-made cabinets available, beware of so-called "budget" cabinets that are almost shoddy even while still new, held together partly with wire staples in knock-down pieces to be assembled, shelves supported on pins instead of being securely recessed into dadoes, and in some instances with a coverup coating of thick stain in place of a lasting finish.

If you resurface your existing cabinets with plastic laminate, you may find it worthwhile to build one or two new ones for special purposes—a wall oven, for example—or a replacement to allow space for installing a dishwasher. You can build a new sink countertop yourself with a laminated plastic surface, or go all out by making and installing a luxurious Corian marble-like counter that is warm, attractive and almost indestructible.

Step-by-step instructions for building each type of cabinet are given in subsequent chapters, including details on making the utility connections.

In the past, the biggest problem in making cabinets at home was finishing them with lacquer or enamel, which required extensive equipment, considerable expertise, a place to do that kind of work—and much patience. Finishing no longer is a problem; plastic laminate sheeting, applied with contact cement, assures a perfect, care-free surface. The thin sheeting is lightweight; several panels can be easily rolled into a bundle that fits into your car.

All the cabinets and counters shown here have actually been built by the author in a home workshop. A table saw or radial-arm saw is almost a must for building the cabinets and doing other parts of the kitchen project. A saber saw or portable circular saw will be helpful in various stages of the work, particularly for cutting large plywood panels into more easily handled pieces. A ¼″ electric drill, a spirit level, a long carpenter's square and other basic hand tools also will be required.

Planning the layout is an important part of your kitchen project. You will want to know where every cabinet and appliance will go, so new cabinets can be built with the assurance they will fit and that no space factor has been overlooked. There are many sources for help in planning. Every appliance dealer has illustrated booklets prepared by appliance and cabinet manufacturers; some offer layout charts which can be obtained free. Make sure you get the manufacturer's specifications and dimensions for the appliances you plan to install.

Ralph Treves

11 | Rejuvenating Existing Cabinets

BEFORE YOU DECIDE to buy or build new cabinets for your kitchen, consider the practical options for refurbishing the existing cabinets. They may be out of style and show signs of wear, or possibly you're just tired of their appearance and want a change. Very likely, however, those cabinets are structurally sound and perfectly serviceable. If so, you can give them a facelift by resurfacing with attractive, stainproof, amazingly durable laminate (of which Formica and Consoweld are well-known brands) in your preferred color and pattern. However, if you prefer a natural wood finish, resurface the cabinets with ⅛-inch hardwood-veneered plywood instead of plastic laminate.

One major benefit of this rejuvenation method is that it causes only minimum fuss in the household with little disruption of family routines, and it's not even necessary to empty the cabinets. Important, too, is that this work can be done piecemeal, in your spare time.

New-style square-edged doors and drawer fronts, faced with the same plastic or plywood, help set the modern tone, making your kitchen more pleasant and efficient, even increasing the value of your home because of its up-to-date look.

When the plastic sheeting is put up and neatly trimmed, the job is done—no further surface finishing is required and the easy-to-clean cabinets will stay fresh-looking for years. A wood veneer surface, however, will need to be stained and the surface sealed with clear lacquer or shellac.

RESURFACING WITH PLASTIC. You have several options in planning this work. One is to buy, at home supply centers, standard-size 4'x8' plastic panels, which are flexible enough so that they can be rolled to fit into your car, and cut them to approximate sizes for laminating to the cabinet surfaces with contact cement.

This is the procedure: (1) take down all doors, drawers and any surface hardware; (2) remove the old finish and surface wax (if the finish is enamel, apply paint remover; if clear lacquer over stain, wash down with acetone lacquer thinner); sand the stained surfaces; (3) laminate the plastic sheeting with contact cement, using a paper slip sheet if necessary for positioning; (4) trim excess overhang plastic with a router having a carbide cutter bit; (5) buy or rebuild the doors and drawer fronts in current style, coat with the plastic and reinstall with new hardware. Done!

A much easier—and somewhat more expensive—method is to order factory-built doors and drawer fronts from a local kitchen-cabinet dealer or home supply center, together with plastic pieces cut to precise dimensions for resurfacing

Old-style cabinets with painted doors, lacking interest and character but otherwise in sturdy condition, can be renewed with plastic surfacing and new doors.

Same cabinet surfaced in colorful wood grain with easy-to-clean plastic laminate. Doors are square-edged, overlapping the cabinet face with modern spring-loaded hinges and attractive door pulls. Note new plastic-surfaced countertop and desk.

the exposed areas of the cabinets. The doors come with matching plastic laminated to the outside surface, a neutral color plastic on the inside, edges neatly banded all around with a narrow plastic.

Take precise measurements of your cabinet openings. When ordering, show on a sketch where each door is located and which direction it swings, so that provision can be made for clearance, particularly when two doors are adjacent in the same cabinet. Also, measure accurately all exposed cabinet surfaces that are to be covered. The pieces that are provided by the dealer will be of the exact sizes ordered—unless you request a ¼-inch or so overage for trimming with a router bit. Router trimming is recommended as it would be extremely difficult to fit all the pieces precisely.

First step in resurfacing: Old doors are discarded, cabinet surfaces stripped of old paint, sanded smooth. Plastic panels are put on the cabinet sides, front edges trimmed.

Front cabinet members are surfaced with strips of the same plastic, applied with contact cement, then trimmed with router.

Mitered strip is marked with a try square, cut with tin snips to form tight fit with adjacent strip. The tedious cutting and fitting of small pieces can be avoided by full-panel application shown later in this chapter.

New doors are made of ⅝-inch chipboard, faced two sides with the plastic laminate. One way to speed this up is to laminate half a panel at a time, then slice it into the required door widths.

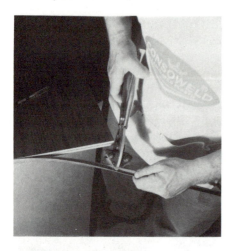

Door edges are square, trimmed with either the strips of the same plastic ripped to required width, or with a heavy T-shaped plastic in neutral color.

Be sure to predrill for hinge screws; otherwise they may move slightly when driven and may distort hinge position.

Efficient modern door hinges are spring-loaded for self-closing. Doors are easily hung because they simply overlap the cabinet openings all around, but make sure they're all hung uniformly.

One-piece coverage. Here's a better way of doing the laminating easily and neatly: Instead of cutting the plastic panel into precisely sized pieces and fitting each into place, apply the uncut plastic in one piece over the entire area of each surface that is to be done. With a mallet, tap the plastic at all points to secure good bonding. Then drill a ⅜-inch hole in one inside corner. This permits inserting the router bit, which will cut through to one side of the open section. Draw the router along the inside cabinet rails—the guide on the bit will stay on a straight course. Continue all around, cutting out the waste piece of plastic.

Follow this procedure at all cabinet openings, including the drawer spaces. Do the exposed sides of each cabinet first, routing the outside edges smooth, then apply the front panel with its edges overlapping the outside corners slightly. Finally, trim with the router. The technique of cementing the plastic is discussed later in this chapter.

One problem you must cope with is that the router bit does not cut squarely into the corners. You might have to use a special carbide-tipped scriber, backing the corner material with a block of wood while the excess material is cut square. The trick in doing this is to scribe the piece on both sides of the corner, then make a straight cut across the center. This permits breaking out the two parts of the rounded corner. Don't attempt to cut this piece out with a saw, as chipping may result.

There is a certain technique for handling the plastic sheeting. Always cut with a fine-toothed blade, on a bench saw or by hand, but be sure always that the cutting is done with the blade teeth entering through the finish (plastic coated) facing; otherwise there will be considerable chipping—thus, when cut on a bench saw, the panel is placed facing up. Also, when using a carpenter's or dovetail saw, have the teeth biting into the plastic directly. But with a saber saw, or hack saw, the cutting must be done in reverse, the face side down. Cut the panels at least ¼-inch oversize, allowing the panel to be adjusted squarely on the surface.

Instead of cutting small sections to fit the cabinet front, use a single large piece to cover the entire surface. Then use a router, with special carbide trimmer bit, to cut away the excess and smooth the edges neatly all around the inside openings.

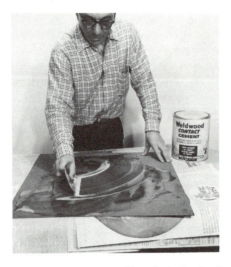

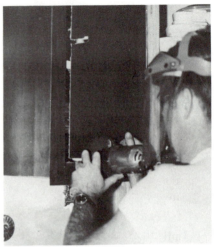

Apply contact cement liberally to back of each panel section, spreading the cement evenly with a piece of hardboard. Make sure every spot is covered. Allow to dry thoroughly, while you apply the cement to the cabinet surfaces. Touch with a piece of kraft paper to determine when fully dry.

Plastic sheet has been cemented to the front of the cabinet. Now router bit is inserted through drilled hole at corner to cut away excess.

Most of the excess has been cut away. The outside corner is neatly trimmed, the front sheet overlapping the edge of the side panel. The large sheet that has been cut out can be used for door facings or drawer fronts.

Some of the larger pieces that are removed by the routing can be used for door facings or drawer fronts, thus reducing waste. This method creates an integral, unbroken surface, rather than one with many narrow strips on the rails and uprights, which at best would not always be perfectly joined. Be careful always to avoid chipping the plastic, however slightly.

Your cabinet doors most likely have bullnose edges, which has been the prevailing style for several decades. Doors today are square-edged; they are hung with spring-loaded hinges, have magnetic catches for no-effort closure, and door edges that overlap the cabinet sides all around. It wouldn't be practical to cut down the bullnose edges; the doors would then be too small. It's better to make new doors of ½-inch or ⅝-inch chipboard. Coat the door on both sides with a laminate (for uniform tension) and band the edge with a narrow plastic strip or veneer. Preferred is a T-shaped plastic strip fitted into a deep groove all around.

Adapting the drawer fronts. The drawers present a different problem, as it wouldn't be practical to disassemble the drawer and change the front. It's easier to cut away the overhang on the existing drawer front, so that the new drawer front can be attached to the old one. Cutting away the overhang permits the drawer to be pushed in deeper, so the new facing will come up flush with the cabinet itself.

Trimming the drawer front is best done on a table saw, the drawer held upright to slide alongside the fence so that the sides are cut away flush with the drawer sides, except that the top must be cut down to the level of the drawer sides. The trimming need not be perfectly neat as the new facing will cover any imperfections. While you have the drawers out, it's a good idea to drill four small holes in the front for the screws that will attach the new facing.

The drawer fronts must be level; if one or more is askew it will be very obvious. Apply a coating of adhesive cement before attaching the new drawer fronts to the original trimmed ones, but make certain first that the drawer goes in far enough to allow fitting the new facing.

Old drawer front must be trimmed flush (dotted line) before attaching new front. Then drawer can be pushed in deeper, allowing new front to contact cabinet face.

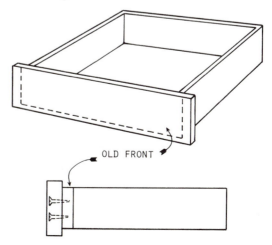

OLD FRONT

WOOD SURFACING. If you prefer real wood instead of a plastic surface, you can proceed as previously described using thin hardwood-veneered plywood. It may be necessary to make new square-edged doors which also are veneered. Sand the edges smooth and finish with stain, then coat the surface with shellac or clear lacquer. Steps in resurfacing with plywood are shown at right.

BASIC PROCEDURE. Use standard contact bond cement, available in cans from half-pint to gallons. Spread the cement on both surfaces to be bonded; the back of the plastic panel and the cabinet surfaces. Apply sufficient cement to cover completely, spread with a piece of hardboard. Make certain there are no skipped spots.

Allow both parts to dry, which will take about twenty minutes at room temperature (you can test this with a piece of kraft paper—if it tends to stick, the cement is still not sufficiently dry). You will need a piece of heavy kraft paper large enough to cover the biggest area that will be laminated. This is a "slip sheet" that helps position the plastic correctly. Remember that the plastic bonds "on contact" and can't be shifted around. The illustrations show how this slip sheet is used.

Place the plastic sheet in position and square it up with the cabinet (as the plastic will be a bit oversize, allow an overlap at the front edge). Bend the plastic up slightly at one end and fold the paper inward, then press down on the plastic—it will bond in place instantly.

Lift the other end, draw out the paper entirely, and press down the rest of the plastic, which should now be in alignment, covering the exposed part of the cabinet. Tap with a rubber mallet or hammer on a small block of wood covering every part to assure a firm bond. If properly done, the plastic will be securely and permanently attached. Trim off the excess overhang that has been provided by running a router along the edge. Some booklets suggest filing off this edging, but the result obtained in that manner is seldom satisfactory and there is considerable chance of chipping a plastic edge with the file.

The router bit used to trim the plastic must be the carbide type; otherwise it will quickly be dulled by the hard, brittle melamine plastic.

Hardwood veneered plywood in ⅛-inch thickness is applied over the old surface. Sides are covered first, edges sanded, as they will be overlapped by the front panel.

Plywood strips are easily cut on a circular saw. Use a sharp blade so edges will be clean and smooth. Keep the good side face up on the saw table.

Spread contact cement on backs of plywood strips; also coat the cabinet face. Allow the cement to dry thoroughly.

The front strip is placed flush with the edge of the cabinet so there will be a neat, tight-fitting joint. Tap on a wood block with a mallet to assure perfect bonding.

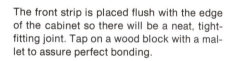

12 | **Building Base Cabinets**

ALTHOUGH THE dimensions of base cabinets have hardly varied over the years, there have been many advances that should be kept in mind and incorporated, if possible, into the cabinets that you are building. You surely want to have the up-to-date conveniences that have been developed by clever designers, including easy-glide drawers, self-closing doors, easy-to-clean and durable plastic surfaces.

Base cabinets are those that stand directly on the floor, in contrast to wall-hung cabinets or those that rest on other surfaces. There are several forms of base cabinets: freestanding; undercounter cabinets that provide support for sink inserts and drop-in tabletop stoves; corner cabinets; tall wall-oven cabinets; broom closets and even desks—the last having come to be regarded as an almost essential kitchen fixture.

The depth of a base cabinet is usually 24″, measuring from the finished front of the cabinet frame—not counting the doors or drawer fronts—back to the wall. This modular depth allows for installing an appliance, such as a dishwasher or compactor, flush with the front. The countertop, however, has an overhang of 1″ at the front so the counter is usually made 25″ deep, with a vertical splash at the back wall.

Height of the base cabinet is a standard 34½″, which with the countertop brings the total height to 36″, generally regarded as the most convenient working height for most people. If a lower level would be more comfortable for you, make the adjustment for height in designing the cabinet. However, this may necessitate shifting the dishwasher to a separate cabinet—the sink and stove counter inserts will fit regardless of the cabinet. The other needed dimensions are indicated on the sketch opposite.

The 25″ depth of the countertop allows for making a cutout 21″ or 22″ deep for installing the sink; the undersink cabinet should be planned to allow for this insert, making sure that no cross member or upright is in the way.

One base cabinet shown is 5′ wide, designed to fill the area between a dishwasher and the corner wall oven. The step-by-step instructions that follow for building this cabinet apply also to similar construction.

The cabinet is built of ¾″ plywood or particleboard (the ⅝″ panel thickness is sometimes preferred as it is lighter and more easily handled, provides an almost equally solid construction). The cross rails and front facings also can be made of remaining pieces of the plywood, or solid lumber stock used for the purpose.

The 5′ cabinet supports a countertop which will contain the drop-in stove, so space is provided in its interior to accommodate the stove depth and its controls. The stove depth varies with each make, so it's advisable to obtain those dimen-

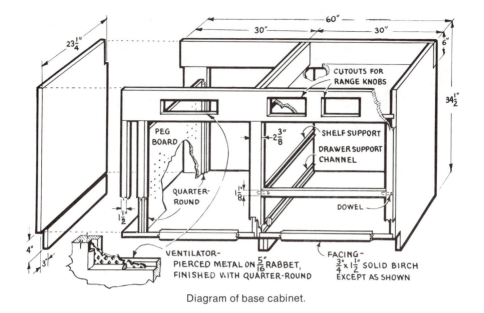

Diagram of base cabinet.

sions when planning the cabinet. Another important detail is that a sufficient space be provided between the stove burner and the nearest flammable wall surface on that side. A minimum of 15″ is usually required for safety and must be allowed for in the design of the base cabinets.

Construction starts with cutting the uprights, including the center partition, standard 34½″ high, and 23¼″ front to back. With the addition of the ¾″ thick facing frame at the front, total depth will be 24″.

Clamp the uprights together and cut out the 3″ x 4″ toe space. Also cut a notch in the upper rear corner of each upright to fit a 6″ cross rail of 1″ stock across the back. The range section of the cabinet will have a shelf to enclose the space 10″ deep under the range. To do this, cut dadoes ¼″ deep at each end to locate that shelf in the side upright and center partition. Then cut the dadoes for the bottom shelves. At each step in construction, use a large square to check right angles.

1. First step in assembly is to fasten rail at rear of uprights. Use try square at every step of the assembly.

2. Shelves surfaced with plastic laminate are slipped into dadoes cut in uprights to help square up cabinet.

3. Cutout for sink ventilator and range control knobs is marked on front facing. Cutout size is in manufacturer's specifications.

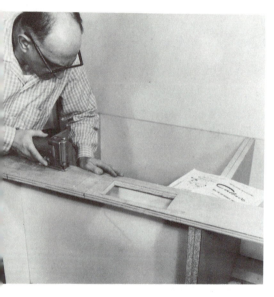

4. Saber saw is used to make the cutouts for control knobs and sink ventilator. Holes are drilled at corners to start saw blade. After cutting is finished, file is used to square up the corners.

5. Front facing is applied.

The front facing is of ¾″ plywood. If the stove has front controls, the facing strip will have to be relatively wide: if the stove controls are in the countertop, the strip can be narrower, or a drawer fitted in place of the controls. Make the cutouts for spacing the controls before assembling the cabinet.

If the cabinet is intended for placement under the sink, no shelf is included, just the bottom panel. Allow clearance for a drainpipe and trap, plus a grinder unit with dishwasher connections, if these appliances will be included.

6. Trim strip is fastened to lower shelf of cabinet with glue and finishing nails. Strip can have top edge flush with upper surface of bottom shelf, or with lower surface so that lip is formed.

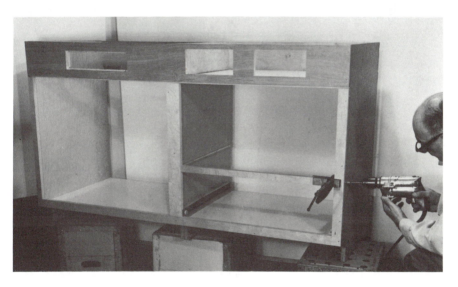

7. Horizontal separator strips are clamped between blocks that also are clamped to vertical strips, so they are flush with each other. Holes are drilled through edges and ends for dowels.

To assemble, attach the rear cross rail in its notches with screws. Next, attach the plywood front facing strip with finishing nails or brads through the face, or with screws through blocks on the back that are glued and screwed to the vertical members. Now, slide the shelves into their dadoes and drive screws into their edges through the vertical members, or use glue. No back panel is used on the cabinet; the kitchen wall provides the back. A strip is now fastened across the front edge of the lower shelf, its top edge flush with the upper surface of the bot-

8. Completed base cabinet with doors in place.

tom shelf, or its lower edge flush with the bottom of the shelf, forming a lip. The vertical strips are 1½″ wide, except for the center strip, which is 2⅜″ wide to cover the center partition (because of the double door hinges). Horizontal strips between drawer openings are 1⅛″.

Fasten the horizontal strips to the verticals with glued ¼″ dowels. When drilling holes through the vertical members, wrap a piece of electrical tape around the drill as a depth stop. Clamp a block of wood to the front and back of the vertical and horizontal strips to keep them flush with each other while you drill.

The basic cabinet now is complete and should stand solidly and level on the floor. All that remains is to install drawer runners, doors, drawers and hardware.

When installing the cabinet, check to make sure it is plumb and level before attaching to the back wall. It may be necessary to shim up the base, or trim the lower ends of the vertical members of the cabinet, to get it plumb and level. If this cabinet is to be joined with others, the fronts must be aligned flush, clamped and bolted. Enclosing the toe space is done last, a single strip being used to cover the toe space for two or more cabinets in a line.

To install a base cabinet, either rip away the baseboard or cut notches in the lower rear corners of the uprights so the units can be pushed against the back wall in alignment. Measure 34½″ from the floor at several points on the wall and draw a level line as a guide for fastening the cabinets through their top rails. Then drill a series of holes in each rail.

124

13 | Corner Cabinet with Rotary Shelves

An L-shaped corner cabinet design with access to rotating shelves has evolved to solve a two-fold problem: making convenient use of otherwise wasted space deep in the corner, tying together in a practical manner two cabinets that meet at right angles and utilizing as a work surface the large corner countertop spanning the double cabinets.

The revolving shelf system works well, providing efficient, easy-to-reach storage space for canned goods, cleaning supplies, extra jars and other necessities.

This corner arrangement permits a single stretch of counter to extend across the top of both cabinets. The revolving unit is a standard Lazy Susan kit consisting of two pie-shaped metal shelves with hubs to fit a vertical center tube, to which the shelves are locked at convenient levels with set screws. The cabinet shown has two narrow doors at front, at right angles, mounted directly on and revolving with the shelves. The shelves are 22″ in diameter.

Diagram of corner cabinet.

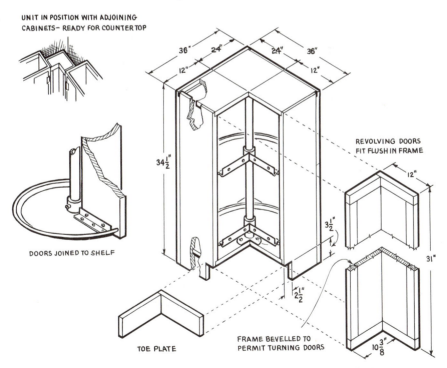

UNIT IN POSITION WITH ADJOINING CABINETS— READY FOR COUNTER TOP

DOORS JOINED TO SHELF

36″ 24″ 24″ 36″

12″ 12″

$34\frac{1}{2}$″

REVOLVING DOORS FIT FLUSH IN FRAME

12″

$3\frac{1}{2}$″

31″

$2\frac{1}{2}$″

TOE PLATE

FRAME BEVELLED TO PERMIT TURNING DOORS

$10\frac{3}{8}$″

To reach the shelves, either door is pushed inwardly, thus rotating the shelves and bringing all items into reach. You might even have a small electric bulb lighting the interior when the doors are opened.

The cabinets are both built so front edges are flush with adjacent cabinets. Thus the sides are 24″ deep, but both panels are 36″ wide to fit all the way into the corner, clearing the 12″ wide center opening. The revolving doors are 10⅜″ wide.

Start by ripping a 3′ width from a ¾″ 4′ x 8′ plywood panel, then saw this piece to get two 34½″ lengths. These will serve as the backs of the cabinets. Rip another 4′ x 8′ panel in half to get two 2′ widths; saw one piece to get two 34½″ lengths, which will be used for the sides. You will also need two pieces of ¾″ plywood, each cut first to 3′ x 3′ size for top and bottom members. In both, one corner, 12″ x 12″, is cut away. One piece is used for the top of the cabinet, fitted into rabbets cut in the top edge of the sides, the other is for the bottom shelf, this one held in dado slots in the sides. Possibly the latter will be slightly shorter in each dimension and should be trimmed to fit. The bottom front corner of each 2′-wide side is notched 2½″ for the toe plate.

In all four uprights (the sides and backs) cut rabbets ⅜″ deep and ¾″ wide, at the top, for joining the plywood top. Before assembling the cabinet, attach the pole hub for the revolving shelf to the underside of the top, setting the hub directly at the corner of the recess. Now join the cabinet parts, using glue and nails.

Attach short pieces of 1″ x 1″ metal angles—brass or aluminum—with rivets along the pie-shaped opening of the metal revolving shelves. Assemble the Lazy Susan rotating unit inside the cabinet, with the shelf hubs loose, and insert the

1. Cut a dado 3½″ from bottom edge of each side panel to receive bottom shelf. This measurement can be altered to suit personal preference or to match other cabinets. Then cut rabbet at other end.

2. Reduce the width of one cabinet back ¾″, then drill screw holes in back and in edge of side panel.

pole into the hub at the top. The bottom hub is fastened in place with screws so the pole is plumb. Tighten setscrews in shelf hubs to lock them at the desired heights. Test to see that the shelves rotate smoothly.

The doors are made next, of either solid wood or ¾" plywood. Cut the doors to size. One is approximately 10⅜" x 31", the other ¾" wider for the overlap. Bevel the side edges to allow clearance as the shelves rotate and the doors disappear inside the cabinet. Attach these doors to the metal angles on the shelves with screws—there will be access to do this from the inside.

Surfacing of this L-shaped cabinet top with a single section of plastic sheeting is described in Chapter 11.

3. Attach the back to cabinet sides, using a try square to keep the joint square while driving screws. Temporarily fitting the top member helps to keep the sides true.

4. With the top temporarily in place, mark the lines for the setback cutout in both top and bottom shelves.

5. With the setback cut out, install the bottom shelf in its dado. If fit is snug, tap shelf into place with a mallet. Glue can be used in assembly.

6. Revolving-shelf hardware (above) comes as a set. Attach baseplate at corner of bottom cutout. Metal circular shelves can be purchased or wooden shelves cut to fit.

7. Attach facing strip with finishing nails and countersink heads (right).

8. Angles can be attached to pie cut made in circular metal shelves using screws (above) or rivets (above r.) and doors attached to the angles (right).

The completed corner cabinet aligned with its adjacent base cabinet.

14 | **Wall Cabinets**

WALL CABINETS ARE usually smaller and lighter than base units. Dimensions vary according to location, some as shallow as 12″ where space is limited. Those above the sink and countertop should allow plenty of clearance to avoid head injury, while any cabinet above the range must leave sufficient distance to avoid fire hazard.

It would seem preferable to build the cabinets as tall as possible for maximum storage space, even if the top shelves can be reached only with a step stool. But appearance is important, too, and decorators favor keeping cabinet height to reasonable limits. A soffit can fill the gap neatly between cabinets and ceiling.

Here are some rules-of-thumb for planning the clearances of kitchen wall cabinets:

Over the work counter: 15″ clearance when cabinets are approximately 12″ deep; 20″ when cabinets are up to 18″ deep.

Above the stove: 28″ clearance, permitting installation also of a combination range hood and exhaust fan.

Over the sink: 30″ clearance (at least).

Limit the wall cabinet widths to 36″, sufficient for double doors. This keeps the shelf span within proper limits, avoids buckling under excessive weight.

Diagram of a typical wall-hung cabinet. This one is 33¾″ wide; maximum width is 36″.

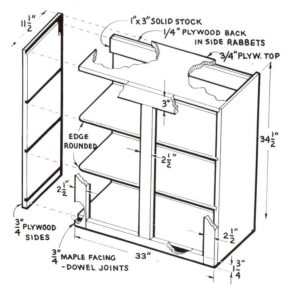

Whether the cabinet is anywhere from 12″ to 36″ high, framing details are generally the same, as shown by the sketch. Interior surfaces may be finished with plastic sheeting, laminated to the parts before assembly, while the exterior is either a hardwood veneer or plastic, laminated to the surfaces after the unit is completed but before hanging. The unit shown in the illustrations has front facings of ¾″ solid maple. The back panel is ¼″ plywood. The dimensions shown in the sketch are, of course, for illustration purposes only.

Cabinets must be hung securely because they carry considerable weight in dishes, glassware, etc. Attaching the cabinet to the wall by means of the back panel alone is treacherous. A suggestion for safety with the design shown is a wood rail fitted to the back of the cabinet, recessed under the top panel so that it can be securely attached to the wall to bear the full weight of the cabinet.

Additional screws or nails are placed into the top or sides wherever there is a good purchase. While support rails under the cabinet are generally regarded as unsightly, such rails can be disguised in many ways—for example, to simulate wainscoting or a panel divider. At any rate, build your cabinets sufficiently strong so the bottom won't pull away or leave the wall.

Another detail: Don't make the cabinet of precise height to fill the space— leave at least ½″ clearance because the ceiling or soffit may be uneven. The gap is later covered with a cove or crown molding along the front that "ties" the line of cabinets together.

Vary the shelf positions in different cabinets to serve specific purposes. Set shelves securely into side rabbets or drill the side panels for adjustable brackets.

Make certain that the cabinet sides are square when clamping them for glue pressure. Four pipe clamps are needed for the glue operation, with wood pressure plates under the clamp heads. Wipe off squeeze-out glue with a damp cloth.

It's easier to fit and attach the doors while the cabinets are flat on a workbench, but remove the doors before hanging to reduce the weight. Replace the door hinges in the previous holes once the cabinet is hung. Apply cove molding across the top, spanning several cabinets in a line. Miter the inside or outside corners.

1. Mark off locations of dadoes for shelves on inner surfaces of the side members.

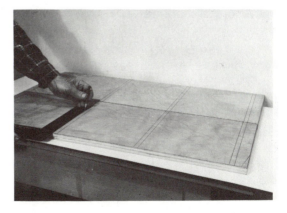

2. To cut dadoes on a radial saw, cut along marked lines first, then shift stock slightly between passes.

3. Cut a mortise ¾'' by 3'' under top dado. This is for cross rail that is used as a hanging bar.

4. Apply glue to all dadoes using a small brush in order to spread the adhesive uniformly and to reach the corners.

5. Assemble the cabinet by installing shelves, top and bottom, in the dadoes. Attach the cross brace with glue and screws to the sides; then nail (or screw) it through the top.

6. Nail face frame to cabinet and drill holes through edges to dowel-joint the center piece, for added strength.

7. Use a bar clamp to draw side members of cabinet against top, bottom and shelves; top and bottom of facing against the center piece.

8. Before installing cabinet, locate wall studs and framing of soffit. Drill clearance holes through plasterboard.

9. Lift the cabinet in place and drive a nail through cross brace into the studs. This will hold cabinet in place while you drive other nails and screws as needed.

10. Cabinet installed with trim in place. Now you can re-hang the doors, which had been removed before hanging the cabinet.

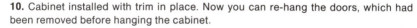

15 | Wall Oven Cabinet

BUILT-IN WALL ovens have won wide acceptance for easy access without bending, in addition to their attractive modern appearance. The efficient self-cleaning and continuous-cleaning feature in either gas or electric models is of course a splendid achievement, much welcomed. An array of practical and dependable control devices also help to assure perfect culinary results.

The sketch showing construction details of a wall oven cabinet, of ceiling or soffit height, includes a large storage space above the oven and a deep drawer underneath for roasting pans and other bulky kitchen equipment. When the oven is located adjacent to a tabletop stove, be sure to leave at least 15″ between the nearest burner and the cabinet wall.

An important consideration for the homeowner planning a complete kitchen modernization is that the wall oven need not be a part of the "sink-stove-counter" work center; if the room arrangement requires it, the oven may be lo-

Wall oven, completed and installed, is a pleasure to use. Both gas and electric types are available in self-cleaning and continuous-cleaning models.

cated on another wall, even recessed into a partition wall backing into another room; or partway into the lower segment of a closet wall, taking up only a small part of the closet. The back of the oven is, of course, fully boxed in and not visible. Sides of the cabinet are of ¾″ plywood, ripped from a 4′ x 8′ panel, and joined with shelves into deep dadoes or supported on cleats. (One shelf is made extra sturdy to support the heavy oven.) The front facings match those of other cabinets. The utility lines—gas and electric—are brought in from the back.

The wall cabinet must be wide enough to receive the oven, allowing for the thickness of the side panels. But don't measure too closely—you'll want some side clearance for ease of installation. Any wall gap will be neatened with corner molding. Gas ovens must be front-vented.

Constructing the oven cabinet. When measuring the space for locating a corner oven cabinet, don't rely on a single reading, as corner walls are rarely square and plumb. Take measurements at top, bottom and several points between, accepting only the narrowest dimension.

The construction starts with ripping the two sides from a 4′ x 8′ plywood panel, so each half is 23¼″ wide. If your table saw is not able to handle the full-size panel, do the ripping along a guide line with a portable circular saw or even a carpenter's hand saw, as this cut can be made "rough." No need to worry about keeping a perfect edge because the factory-cut outside edges can be used for the front of the cabinet.

Sketch shows details of average oven cabinet, though dimensions and specifications vary according to the particular brand and model. Oven dimensions and utility connections are specified in installation leaflet supplied by manufacturer.

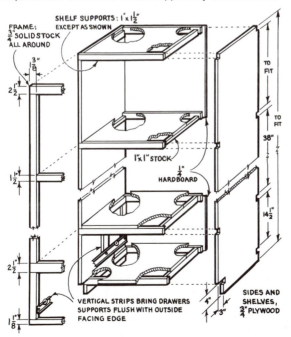

The two pieces are then sawed to correct length to fit the space. Don't try to crowd the full length to the ceiling because it would be impossible to raise the completed cabinet—rather, make the cabinet short enough to allow for sufficient ceiling clearance; later you will close the space at the top of the cabinet with crown molding.

Keep in mind the position of this cabinet. Even though it goes into a corner, one side may be visible, at least in part over an adjacent base cabinet. The visible part can be faced with plastic laminate to match the rest of the cabinets. The laminate is particularly advantageous alongside the cook stove as it is impervious to splattered grease, but be sure there is adequate distance from the burners of at least 15″. The plastic can be added after the cabinet is built.

After the panels are cut to length, provide grooves and notches as needed for the cross members, the shelf supports, the backing panels and front facings, according to the sketch. Cut the toe space at the bottom corners uniform with the other cabinets, 4′ high and 3″ deep; also cut back the rear corners if the baseboard will not be removed for clearance. At the top of the toe recess, cut a 1″ x 1½″ slot in both sides for a shelf support cross member. Make additional slots in the front edge of the plywood at the two positions as shown, above and below the oven location.

The oven should be located at a convenient height. This depends on the type, whether it has a separate broiler section, or has just the oven-broiler combination compartment. If there is a separate broiler under the oven section, the recommended height is 21″ above the floor. Thus the top of the support slot will be 20¼″ above the floor, which allows for the thickness of the shelf itself. The

1. Start cabinet construction by ripping plywood panel down the center. Place both panels together, with original factory edge on same side. Cut the front toe-space first. A portable saber saw does this in minutes.

2. Cut slots for the supporting cross members that join the uprights and also serve as shelf supports. Install the crossmembers and also attach the shelf rails at same positions, across the panels, with screws.

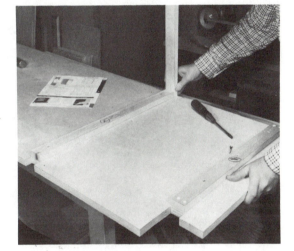

3. Screw 1″ x 1½″ shelf supports to the uprights.

space for the oven between this shelf and the one above it depends on the specifications of the oven you will use, as indicated on its installation sheet.

In addition to these cross-members, the shelves are supported by 1″ x 1″ rails on both side panels and the backing panel.

Before assembly, attach the metal slides for the lower drawers as it is easier to line them up while the panels are flat, side-by-side.

Assemble the basic cabinet by joining the cross members, the shelf rails, and backing panels of ¼″ hardboard nailed to the uprights.

There is no backing panel at the center section behind the oven because the space must be kept open for the gas and electric connections, but the top and bottom compartments may be enclosed. Shelves are cut to fit and securely fastened above the cross members. These shelves may be painted if desired, but the best finishing is to cover them on both sides with the same plastic as on the countertops. If you have any leftover pieces of the plastic this is the place to use them.

The front facing strips are attached with glue and headless brads, which are countersunk and the holes filled with wood putty.

The gas or electric connections are roughed in before the cabinet is raised upright. The open back at the center space permits final utility hookups before the oven is installed.

4. Front facings consist of ¾″ solid birch strips, sold by mail-order firms. Facings should be square at all corners, so doors and drawers will fit. The electric box and gas lines are "roughed in" as described later.

16 | Basic Drawer Construction

DRAWERS FOR KITCHEN cabinets are basically similar in construction; differences are mostly in the details. Current style calls for square-edged facings, the drawers moving smoothly on nylon rollers in metal channels, rather than sliding between wood guides that formerly swelled or shrunk with the weather. Surface treatment, such as embossed moldings and veining grooves, plus decorative variations and attractive new hardware, determine the finished appearance of the drawer.

Preferred material for the drawer fronts is hardwood stock, such as maple, poplar or birch, approximately ½″, ¾″ or ⅝″ thick. Sides and backs of drawers are ⅜″ or ½″ solid stock, the bottoms are ¼″ or ⅜″ plywood or hardwood, smooth surfaced for easy cleaning.

Keep drawer openings to uniform size where possible. Then you can make a dozen drawers by first cutting all the components. There are many steps and saw-setting changes when making a drawer, so cut all the pieces of one size at the same time. Make one complete drawer first as a model for cutting and grooving all the rest of the components to be sure they'll fit correctly.

Have on hand the metal drawer slides that are to be used, so you can allow for proper clearance at sides or bottom, according to the manufacturer's instructions.

There are several ways to build a drawer. The traditional method is to join the front and sides with dovetail, dado or rabbet joints, or a combination of the last

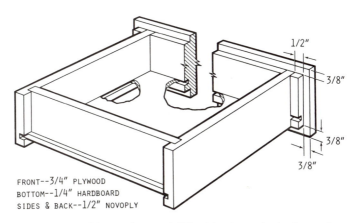

Traditional method of building a drawer. A ⅜″ rabbet is cut in the front all around; then ½″ dadoes are cut to receive the sides and a ¼″ groove is cut for the bottom. Sides are dadoed at rear to receive the back, also grooved for the bottom.

two. The front can overlap the case sides, or it can be made flush with the case sides and concealed by an overlapping false front. The back is usually joined to the sides with dado joints, and the bottom slides into a groove cut in the sides. Variations on this design are shown in the illustrations. Availability of power tools and your own skill usually determine the choice of construction. For maximum strength, dado joints are recommended, but drawers built only with butt joints, glued and nailed, have been known to last many decades.

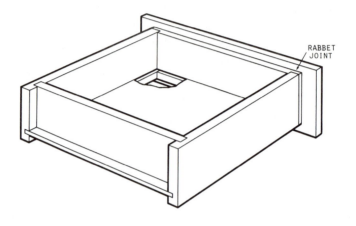

Two other methods of building a drawer: Rather than making the front integral with the drawer, a false front is attached after the basic box frame is built. Above, the front of the box is attached to the sides with rabbet joints; the back and bottom are joined as in the first method. A simpler method is shown below; the box frame is built with butt joints; the bottom rests on ½" strips glue-nailed to the sides.

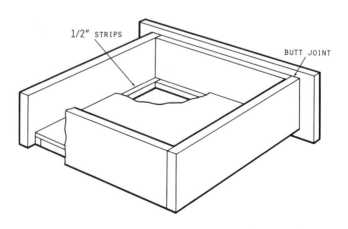

Drawer parts should be glued together under clamp pressure. Place pieces of scrap lumber under the jaws to prevent damage and to distribute the pressure. Start by gluing one side to the front and back, hold lightly with a clamp, then fit in the bottom and finally, the other side. Use two clamps, tightening moderately until the drawer is checked for squareness. Tighten one or the other clamp to bring the assembly to square. After the glue has set, and before removing the clamps, drive a few thin brads into the sides at the front.

Building a drawer by the first method. Dadoes are cut in front to receive sides.

Glue is applied to the dadoes for joining the front with the drawer sides.

Drawer side, which has been dadoed for the back and grooved for bottom, is inserted in front dadoe.

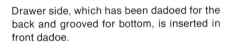

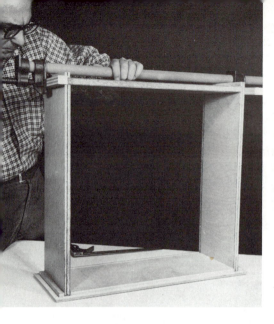
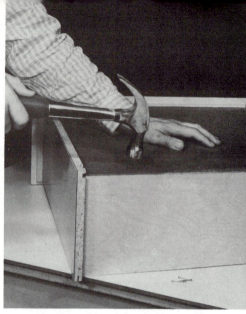

First bar clamp is installed and partially tightened, then bottom is inserted (left). A second clamp is applied at right angles to the first and both tightened moderately until the drawer is square. When glue is dry, bottom is inserted in its groove and is secured to back with brads (right).

Holes for metal slides are drilled in drawer side and slides screwed in place.

Finished drawer being installed in cabinet.

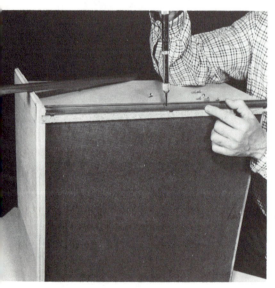

17 | **Countertops**

THE SHAPE OF the countertop need not be determined by the arrangement of the room, as there is considerable leeway in placement of the cabinets. Study the illustrations in shelter magazines and the literature offered by appliance manufacturers to help you set the style. Instructions given here can be adapted to suit any type of counter, whether it is straight, freestanding island, L-shape, rounded-end or your own design.

It's best to have the new countertop completed and ready to install before putting in the base cabinets. Otherwise considerable time would elapse before the sink and drop-in stove could be installed and connected to the utilities. The project will go much smoother if the counter is ready and can be put directly into place on its supporting cabinet, the next major step being to make the counter cutouts for sink and stove.

Remodeled kitchen has counter that contains new sink with one-lever faucet, built-in gas range, and automatic dishwasher under counter. Switch is for garbage disposer.

If possible, the countertop should be a single, continuous unit. Though the base cabinets are separate units, the countertop spans all the cabinets. If the counter distance is longer than the panel from which it is to be made, or the shape is such that it cannot be produced from the single panel, there's a way to join panels invisibly. The fasteners required are described later in this chapter.

Rip a ¾″ plywood or particleboard panel to the width of the countertop, usually 25″, to clear the base cabinet and allow a bit of overhang at the front. If you want to split the panel in half and use one half for the counter, a 1½″-wide strip of the ¾″ plywood can be added along one edge, as the entire counter, including its thickened front edge, will be surfaced with plastic sheet.

Attach 2″-wide strips of ¾″ plywood underneath the counter panel along the front and back edges and on both sides; also place a few similar strips where the counter will rest on the base cabinets, thus preventing any possible sag. The strips serve to double the thickness of the counter at front, giving it a more substantial appearance and the 1½″ added to the base cabinet brings the total height to 36″. If the front edge of the completed counter is to be trimmed with a snap-on metal molding, make provision for the required thickness; otherwise proceed to apply the plastic laminate.

Do the front edge first (also any exposed side edge). Rip strips of the plastic somewhat oversize. The counter will be double ¾″, or 1½″, plus the thin top sheet. But you must also allow a slight excess to be trimmed off with a router, so figure on cutting the strips at least 1¾″ wide. When you have all the strips of proper length, spread contact cement (nonflammable) on both surfaces. Make sure there is complete coverage. Allow to dry thoroughly (about 20 minutes); then put on the strips, carefully aligned. Finally, tap the entire surface with a rubber mallet or a wood block to assure a good bond. Use a portable router with carbide trimmer bit to trim the excess, leaving a perfectly neat edge, top and bottom, of the front plastic.

An alternate method of trimming is to use a sharp plane and a file for smooth finishing, but this method is time-consuming and the result not usually satisfactory.

The process for applying and laminating the large counter sheeting follows specific steps and must be done correctly for a good bond that will not bubble up or loosen at the corners. Do it this way:

Cut the panel to the size and shape of the counter, leaving at least ¼″ excess on all exposed edges. This excess, overlapping the plastic that had been laminated to the front edge, will be trimmed off with the router, as before. (*Note:* If your counter is large or L-shaped, and it won't be possible to cover it with a single sheet of plastic, make the right angle addition separately, including the surface plastic; then join the addition to the main counter section with special fasteners from underneath as described later in this chapter).

Turn the plastic face down and spread the cement over the entire surface. Do the same with the counter panel. Make certain that every spot is covered. Allow both surfaces to dry thoroughly—at least 20 minutes—and test with a piece of the paper to see if the cement is still tacky.

Strip of plywood is attached to front edge of countertop to give thicker appearance. Contact adhesive is brushed on edge and on laminate.

When cement is dry, place laminate strip on counter edge, flush with bottom edge, projecting slightly above countertop to permit trimming.

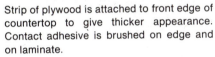

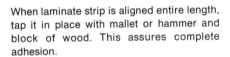

When laminate strip is aligned entire length, tap it in place with mallet or hammer and block of wood. This assures complete adhesion.

Quickest way of trimming laminate is with portable router and laminate-trimming attachment.

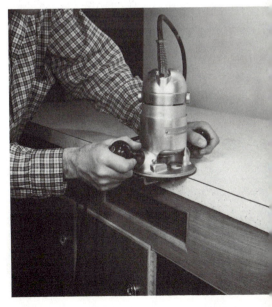

When the panel is dry, cover it with a piece of kraft paper. Put the plastic sheet in place and align the edges with your fingers, the rear edge of the plastic flush with the back of the panel.

Now lift one end of the plastic, fold back the paper about a quarter of the way, then press down. The plastic will adhere to the panel on contact, holding the whole piece in place. Now lift the other end, pull out the paper entirely, press down on the plastic surface. With a rubber mallet, or a hammer and block of wood, tap down on every part of the panel to complete the bond.

The actual trimming goes very quickly. Just run the router bit along the edge smoothly, making sure to hold the router straight so the guide roller rides uniformly along the edge.

Now make the necessary sink and range cutouts, using a saber saw. Mark off the openings directly on the laminate with pencil or crayon. Drill a hole at one corner of each cutout to start the saw. There may be some slight chipping of the plastic, but this will be covered by the sink rim or the range. (Strips of mastic tape on the cutting line will tend to reduce chipping.) Follow the instructions of the manufacturers of the sink and range as to location and clearances required, but make the openings large enough to fit freely. The sink bowl is attached before the countertop is put in place, using a special rim and fasteners, with a heading of caulking putty along the rim.

When the sink is in place, the countertop is installed on the cabinets and pitched so water drains toward the sink. A heavy bowl will cause the top to sag slightly, which helps drainage.

After plastic laminate is applied, cutouts for sink and range are marked directly on surface (left). Be sure all measurements are accurate; use a square to keep guidelines parallel with edge of countertop. Sink rim of aluminum or stainless steel is then positioned on countertop (right) and outlined.

Complete section is saber-sawed from the top, providing for placement of new sink.

Recess in sink rim is packed with plastic glazing compound, then sink bowl is pressed into compound to assure watertight seal between the sink rim and the sink bowl.

Special lugs are spaced around edge of sink bowl, drawn up tight by means of screws so that rim, bowl and countertop are firmly clamped together to make tight joints.

Strips of plywood are used as cross braces under countertop to stiffen it and provide means of attaching top to cabinets by driving wood screws from beneath.

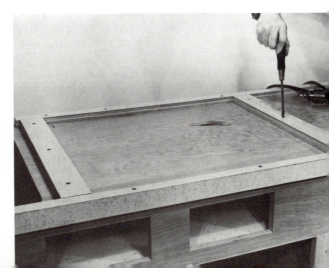

Cove molding is notched to make mitered corner, then is tacked to back edge of countertop to seal joint between countertop and splash board.

CORIAN COUNTERTOPS. A truly elegant touch is added to a kitchen when the counter is made of Corian, which has an attractive opalescent quality with delicately tinted marble veining. The Corian counter presents a very substantial, solid appearance that enhances the entire kitchen.

Corian, made by du Pont, is nonporous, stainproof, heat resistant, and durable. Any minor damage is easily repaired simply by rubbing with a fine-grain sandpaper as the Corian color goes clear through. The latter property permits cleaning with abrasive cleansers, a procedure not recommended for laminated plastics and other surfaces.

Corian is sold by lumber dealers, comes in sheets of 25" width and thickness of ¼", ½" and ¾". The 25" width is perfect for countertops, providing an overhang of 1" beyond the base cabinets. The ¾" thickness is recommended for counters, although the ½" thickness has sufficient solidity to serve for that purpose. (There is a considerable saving in cost and the thinner panel is much lighter, easier to handle.)

Corian can be sawed, drilled and shaped with customary woodworking tools, but they should be of the heavy-duty type, the saw teeth carbide-tipped and kept sharp. This material is exceptionally heavy, the ¾" thickness weighing 14 pounds per running foot in the full 25" width panel. Thus a 10' panel will weigh 140 pounds, so you would need assistance in handling it. You'll probably need a dolly to move it.

Make certain that sawhorses used for support while working are sturdy.

Certain attributes of the Corian are of interest. Contemporary design variations may require jointing of Corian panels for special edge treatment, extra length or various angle shapes. Jointing of Corian is done by gluing or use of fasteners, or other standard jointing measures, including clamping of the joint onto an adhesive-coated length of ¾" particleboard.

The sink cutout can be done with a saber saw, or more quickly, using a portable circular saw, for the straight cuts—but don't be surprised at the quantity of plastic "sawdust" which develops, and should be disposed of promptly and properly. These sink cuts need not be perfectly straight, as they will be covered.

BUTT JOINTS FOR L-SHAPED COUNTERS. The trend toward L-shaped kitchen counters raises the question in many home workshops about how to butt-joint lumber and plywood into the large sizes and shapes.

148

An ingenious fastener developed for this purpose, called Tite-Joint, is sold at most large hardware stores. It draws the edges together for a strong joint with the adjacent surfaces precisely flush on both sides. The edges are drawn together so tightly that the joint is barely visible. No glue is needed, though it can be used for greater strength.

This fastener consists of two circular sleeves, one of which has a round tightening nut, and a special drawbolt. There also is a template that assures accurate drilling of the required holes in the plywood, and a rod for tightening.

This system is particularly excellent for surfaces to be covered with plastic laminate. The photos show how the fasteners are used.

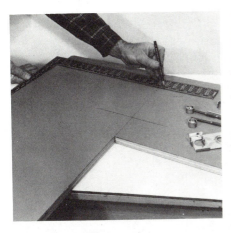

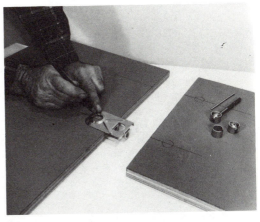

1. Make sure edges of countertop are cut clean and square, with plastic laminate applied. Use square to draw lines across joint 1½″ from each edge to mark location of fasteners.

2. Use drill guide (obtainable with fasteners) to mark positions of the ⅞″ holes that will receive the Tite-Joint sleeves. Guide is designed to provide accurate positioning.

3. Hole is drilled with ⅞″ bit to a depth of just ⅝″. Special drill bit obtainable where fasteners are sold is marked for drilling to the proper depth of ⅝″ to accept sleeves.

4. Position drill guide over drilled hole and clamp in place. Edge of guide now is used to bore 7/16″ holes in edge of stock to receive drawbolts.

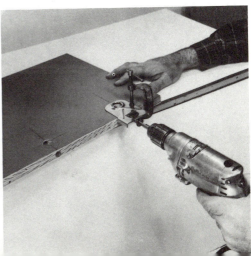

5. Drop collar sleeves with tightening nuts into 7/8″ holes on one side of the joint. Two sections of countertop are placed on flat surface to permit accurate positioning of top surfaces.

6. Push panels together so that drawbolts are engaged by the locking nuts. Shape of locking nuts aligns drawbolts so the threads of the bolts engage threads of the nuts quite easily. Use pin wrench to draw joint together. To prevent twisting and buckling, tighten the nuts uniformly so that pressure is evenly distributed.

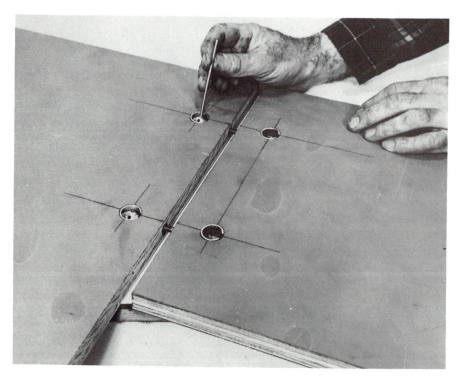

18 | Connecting Kitchen Utilities

ROUGHING IN of the plumbing and electrical connections, also the installation of gas lines where needed, should be scheduled so that these utility installations are made at the most convenient stages in the project—when there is clear access. This way, the project is not halted needlessly later on awaiting these connections.

While doing the basic connections, it will be necessary to shut down the main water valve, the electric system and the gas service. All service doesn't have to be suspended at once, and usually not for long periods, but you'll want to minimize any troublesome complications that will delay getting the household back on normal routine. The techniques for handling each of the utility installations are described and illustrated in detail in the following sections.

The best advice that can be offered is that you do not tackle this work unless you have at least some experience with electrical, plumbing or gas installations, are familiar with the basic requirements and have the mechanical facility needed. Reading up on the subjects will be helpful, but obviously you won't become a skilled plumber or electrician that way. The directions given here, however, will help you to avoid costly errors, and the experience gained as you go along will be valuable and encourage other projects. For family safety, great care must be taken to perform utility work correctly.

In most communities, permits must be obtained by filing specification sheets with a sketch, and the work must be inspected when completed. Be sure to use only approved materials, such as U.L. listed electrical supplies, follow the requirements of the Electrical Code and the standards of the American Gas Association. Some local regulations require that all electrical work be done by licensed electricians, plumbing work done by licensed or qualified plumbers. Gas line installation usually falls into the plumbing category. If you must have the work done by a professional plumber or electrician, you will be able to shave the cost by getting all preparatory work ready, as charges are based on the time spent on the job.

The special tools needed for various stages of the work may not be worth buying for one-time use. Keep in mind that most supply dealers are willing to lend these tools for a limited time to purchasers of materials, usually requiring a deposit. Also in almost every community, tool rental shops have almost every tool that will be needed for the utility connections, at modest rental charges.

For each part of the work, make up a list of materials so you can have on hand everything you need. Lack of a single item can hold up the work for days. For each type of work—plumbing, electricity, gas connections—there are many fittings and parts to meet every conceivable situation. It is impossible to illustrate more than a few, but you can obtain catalogs at dealers or by writing to the manufacturers of required materials.

GAS STOVE AND OVEN CONNECTIONS.

Gas lines for the stove and oven are brought in with iron pipe, ½″ or ¾″ size, joined with threaded fittings, as described elsewhere in this chapter. Whether an existing gas line or a new gas stub, connection from the outlet to the stove and oven is made with special flexible brass tubing of approved design and bearing the American Gas Association (A.G.A) label.

If it is necessary to bring in a new pipe by tapping into a distant existing line, do this by cutting in a T fitting and union coupling rather than starting at the service-entrance meter.

At the stove location be sure to include a shutoff cock in the standpipe at an accessible level, possibly reached through the open back of the base cabinet or other nearby opening. You can also use a smaller diameter pipe than the existing line by including a reducer coupling, down from ¾″ to ½″. Build up the standpipe to required height by adding a nipple topped by a special adapter fitting to take the A.G.A. flexible tubing for connecting to the stove.

When hooking up this tubing, handle carefully to avoid kinking the brass spirals; make certain that the bends are gradual and that tubing is placed so that it

Gas pipe is cut to length that permits installing a T-fitting for a second line extending to the rear of the wall oven (left). Special AGA-rated adapter is fitted on the gas pipe to attach flexible tubing that will connect the gas line to stove or oven (right). Be careful when tightening gas connections not to crack the fittings. Check final assembly connections with soapy water for leaks.

 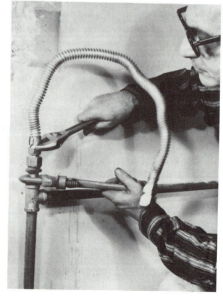

will not be accidentally damaged. The tubing flange nuts are turned with a ¾" or ⅞" open-end wrench. Start the turning by hand, making certain that the threads are not crossed, then draw them up with the wrench so they are just snug tight.

The iron pipe is cut with a special wheeled cutter and threaded with a standard die. But if you have a sketch showing the lengths needed, the dealer can cut and thread the pipe quickly and inexpensively with power equipment. The main tools you will need are two Stillson wrenches, a keyhole saw, a brace-and-bit or a power drill.

After completing the stub line and final connections to the stove and oven, check all joints for leaks, using soapy water with gas turned on.

Test also the operation of the pilot light in both stove and oven, with particular attention to the automatic device in the oven, following the installation instruction sheet of the manufacturer.

PLUMBING CONNECTIONS. Plumbing requirements should be taken into consideration during the planning stage before deciding to shift any appliances, especially the sink. Find out what will be involved in bringing water lines to the new location, and whether there is access to the soil stack and vent for the sink drain, and at a level that allows adequate pitch for draining, without excessive and expensive plumbing work.

Even where the sink will remain in the same spot, a new one may be of different size or its waste outlet in a different position so that line changes are necessary. This will certainly be true if a garbage disposal is added under the sink, or a dishwasher drawing its hot-water line from the sink inlet, its drain emptying into the side of the disposal. There are fittings of every type to meet all possible plumbing needs, so these connections surely can be made, but you should be aware of the problem beforehand. For example, a new location may require breaking into the main soil stack. If the pipe is cast iron, the job should be done by an experienced plumber. Plastic PVC drainpipe is much simpler to work with. The connection can be made by a competent home handyman, the joints sealed with a special cement.

You'll have to decide, at the start, what to use for the water lines—steel pipe, copper tubing or PVC (polyvinyl chloride) pipe. Copper tubing is probably the quickest and easiest to install as it can be bent to fit around obstructions in a continuous length so that a minimum number of fittings are needed, and they are quickly joined by the sweat-soldering method. PVC pipe has been upgraded so it can be used for hot-water inlet lines, but is still generally preferred only for easy drain connections.

When you know where the sink will be, the first stage is roughing in the water line and linking a connection to the drain. The main water valve is closed, hot- and cold-water pipes are brought up through the wall or the floor, to the sink location, approximately in line with the faucet fittings.

Shutoff valves are turned onto the threaded water-inlet pipes, or soldered onto copper tubing. Connection to the faucets is made at each side with a soft

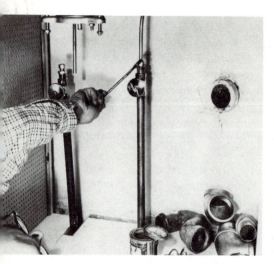

After sink is installed, connections are made to the faucets with adapter tubing and slip nuts from kit that includes shut-off cocks (left). Working in close quarter is easier if pipes are properly aligned. Faucet tubing is soft enough so it can be bent as necessary. Note that drain trap has been temporarily removed until sink is in place. For connecting dishwasher or other appliances, drill through floor (right), bring wiring up behind appliances.

tubing that is supplied with the shutoff valve kit, flexible enough to permit bending to accommodate misalignment.

If there is a dishwasher, it is supplied from a connection tapped off the hot-water line with a special T fitting that is placed into the line below the sink shut-off cock. This line to the dishwasher should have its own valve so that the water can be shut off at any time that dishwasher repairs are needed, without cutting the flow to the sink.

Once the water connections are roughed in, including the shutoff cocks, the main valve may be turned back on to serve the rest of the home, and the sink connections completed at your leisure.

A disposal can be installed under the sink having the necessary 3½″ or 4″ drain opening. Adapters provide for installation in a 5″ opening; the mounting ring and necessary gaskets are supplied with the disposal unit. The drain from the disposal is at a 90-degree angle, leading to the drain trap. A junction box bringing an electrical line for a receptacle to connect the current to the disposal is described in the electrical section.

Dishwasher connections. The dishwasher drain may empty directly into the U trap, or into the disposal by means of a special fitting at the side of the disposal. The anti-vacuum air gap is at the dishwasher end, not at the disposal, which is open at the sink above.

Drain connections usually are not any more complex, if there is a nearby entry to the soil stack at a level that permits an adequate runoff pitch. Always, there is a U trap under the sink, whose purpose is to block entry of sewer gas into the home. This trap is fitted to the outlet from the disposal (or to the sink drain tube) with slip nuts, and joined to the line emptying into the soil stack. When it is necessary to relocate the original drainpipes in the wall, the use of various fittings—nipples and elbows—will bring the drain tube into alignment. Note that with the use of two joined elbows it produces a "swing joint" that allows the drain to swing in an arc on the vertical connection for easy vertical alignment to make the connections.

The dishwasher requires electrical power for the motor, usually ⅓ hp or ½ hp, also for the waste pump, timer, control instruments, and in most current models, heating coils for quick drying. The dishwasher should be powered by a separate appliance circuit, one that has a 20-ampere fuse or circuit breaker. The receptacle may also serve the disposal unit, which may be plugged into the same circuit since it does not draw quite as much current and is operated only for a short period each time.

ELECTRICAL CONNECTIONS. Every one of your kitchen appliances needs electricity, of course. None of these connections, however, is as simple as plugging in a lamp. There are certain considerations that must be given prior attention, particularly whether the existing wall receptacle that you may have been using for years is suitable for the appliances that have been added by the kitchen renovation.

The newer appliances require connection to what is designated as an appliance circuit, one that has a 20-ampere fuse and is wired with sufficient capacity to handle the electrical "current draw" of a major appliance. But you can't upgrade a circuit by changing its fuse to a heavier one—that would be the height of folly: the fuse is an essential safety device in a very powerful energy system with lethal force. A 15-ampere circuit contains No. 14 wire, a 20-ampere circuit has heavier No. 12 wire, while a 30-ampere fuse protects circuits of No. 10 wire. The lower the wire number, the heavier is its gauge or diameter. You can see that the existing fuse represents maximum current capacity of that particular size wire. The resistance put up by undersize wire when there's excessive draw causes overheating of the wire and consequent fire hazard.

If you do need additional appliance circuits, it's not necessary to disconnect the existing receptacles; rather, leave them for other purposes—low current items like clock and radio—and install correct appliance circuits as and where needed.

You can designate the ordinary 15-amp circuit and the 20-amp appliance circuit by various means, such as painting the receptacle covers a specific color, or attaching a dymo-typed tape explaining the usage of the receptacles.

Some heavy-draw equipment is served by twin-wire double circuits, delivering 40 or 60 amperes and 240 volts. These circuits are needed for a water heater, air conditioner, clothes dryer, stove or air conditioner. The receptacles are designed to accept only 3-prong plugs.

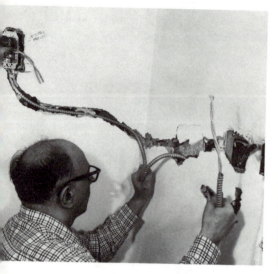

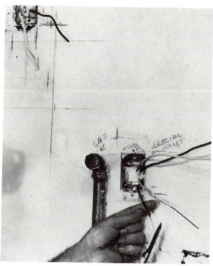

Separate receptacles are provided for oven and for fan in range hood. For electric oven 240-volt line would be required.

Gas and electric lines here are located for the built-in gas oven. Manufacturer's specification sheet gives location.

Electric service installations are done "backwards," that is, the junction or receptacle boxes are roughed in first, the wire connected to the receptacle terminals, the wire cable then snaked back to the circuit box and connected into a circuit breaker or to a fuse block. All splicing of wire must be done within an approved metal junction box, securely fastened to a solid base.

The rule is that each major appliance must have its own individual circuit, but there's a bit of leeway in that a 15-amp or 20-amp line can be tapped off one "leg" of the double circuit. Also, a medium current 20-amp appliance circuit may have a double receptacle. This is not permitted for the heavy current class, such as required for an electric range, clothes dryer or water heater.

Electrical installation is a highly technical procedure, requiring extensive knowledge of regulations and procedures, experience with materials, and skill in working with them. There is no intention here of covering the actual installation of the electrical circuits required in kitchen renovation. Instead, we offer general guidelines to help you avoid a costly and perhaps even a hazardous error.

All stationary appliances must be *grounded*. That means using 3-wire electric cables. The third wire is not insulated and is attached to the green grounding screw of the receptacles. The power end of this bare wire is joined in the circuit box with similar ground wire from other circuits, twisted together and securely attached to the grounding contact screw. Thus in present-day receptacles the third opening is a round hole providing continuity of the ground from the appliance into and through the electrical service box.

If you wish to test the integrity of the ground, use a light bulb in a rubber socket with short wires stripped at the ends. Touch one probe into a side of the receptacle; with the other touch the metal box or metal receptacle cover. If the bulb lights, there is a ground connection; (it's possible that the first side of the receptacle is not the "live side," so try this test on both sides. If there is no result with either side, then the grounding is not complete and should be checked out.

By the way, older receptacles may be easily replaced with the safety grounding type. You can do it yourself by just joining a short wire from the green screw of the receptacle to a screw which would attach the wire to the metal box. Be sure, though, to pull the fuse before taking off the receptacle cover, then check the result to make certain that the grounding continuity has been completed.

A very important safety device that you can easily incorporate into the kitchen installation—and that will serve also for home protection—is a ground fault detector (called GFI for Ground Fault Interrupter). This very sensitive device protects persons using electrical equipment which is "leaking" current onto the appliance frame.

This may occur even in well-made equipment, when the insulation becomes dried out, or some accidental damage causes the live wire to touch the shell and make the appliance "hot." If this occurs with a tool having the 3-prong grounding cord, the current leak will immediately cause a short circuit and blow the fuse. When such an event occurs, do not merely reset the circuit breaker, but rather test each piece of equipment on that circuit to discover the culprit, and correct the cause.

Many appliance cords do not have a 3-prong plug, in particular vacuum cleaners, irons, coffee percolaters, toasters, mixers, fans, can openers and others. But an internal insulation defect is rarely dangerous because the devices are used without touching a ground conductor. If while using the vacuum cleaner you touch a heater pipe, or while plugging in a defective toaster touch a faucet, the result could be a good deal worse than just shocking.

One essential detail that must be given attention is the total capacity of your home electric service. If you've added for the first time a combination freezer-refrigerator, a dishwasher and disposal, perhaps also a window air conditioner or a bench saw for your workshop, the result could well be that the fuses (circuit breakers) keep blowing. The reason is obvious—you just don't have enough electric service in the home to handle the additional load. Recently built homes have 100- or 150-amp service, permitting sufficient individual circuits to handle the various appliances and equipment that have become an essential part of today's home. Older homes with just 60 amps of power—and oft-times even less—were equipped to handle lighting and maybe small accessories like a fan. Although, today's living relies more heavily on electrical power, we have reached a point where we have to reduce our consumption of energy.

The existence of a 3-wire, 240-volt service is not in itself an indication of adequate power source, as the fuses are the determining indicators. If the fuses add up to 60 amps, you won't have much leeway and will require upgrading your service to enjoy the marvelous new equipment that makes life more pleasant and comfortable. But that's only the beginning, as there's not much point to having a 150-amp service and still suffer with the old-time No. 14 and No. 18 wiring that won't handle much more than a table lamp. The solution is new circuits and more of them, all properly grounded.

SAFETY PRECAUTIONS. If you have the proper experience with electrical work, and mechanics generally, it may be possible for you to do much of the new wiring, roughing in wall boxes, connecting the wires to the terminals and to the grounding screws. This work should be done by an experienced electrician or contractor, however, if there's any doubt about your own capability to do a thorough, patient, safe and legal installation.

The prime rule when working with electricity is to "pull the fuse," that is, to disconnect the circuit by turning out the fuse or flipping off the circuit breaker. But the problem is that sometimes the wrong circuit is disconnected, as there's no way of telling just by sight—even the listing on a circuit box card may be incorrect. Best to check out the circuit with a test bulb, or continuity tester, before proceeding.

Another detail of importance is that all wire connections be made really tight, so you're sure they won't be loosened by vibration of the dishwasher or disposal unit, for instance. If the screw does not turn down really tight, remove it and get a new one, and never depend on a terminal screw to support any weight or strain.

Use approved wire cable of the correct size in each installation, comply with all pertinent regulations, avoid used or questionable material, and always maintain the grounding continuity. Attach a separate ground wire from any stationary appliance that does not have a 3-wire grounding plug to a clamp on a sure ground, such as a heater pipe, sanding the pipe surface so there is actual contact of the clamp with the bare metal.

Another word of caution: make it a habit never to touch a faucet or similar conducting surface at the same time that you're plugging in an appliance. Also, for appliances with detachable cords like a percolator, always insert the plug into the appliance before connecting to the receptacle, and vice versa when disconnecting.

Index